The Reorganization of Secondary Education

A Study of Local Policy Making

Philip H. James

Foreword by
Professor Maurice Kogan

NFER Publishing Company

Published by the NFER Publishing Company Ltd.,
Darville House, 2 Oxford Road East,
Windsor, Berks. SL4 1DF
Registered Office: The Mere, Upton Park, Slough, Berks. SL1 2DQ
First published 1980
© Philip H. James, 1980
ISBN 0 85633 2143

Typeset by Datchet Printing Services, Station Approach, Datchet, Berks.
Printed in Great Britain by
King, Thorne & Stace Ltd., School Road, Hove, Sussex BN3 5JE.
Distributed in the USA by Humanities Press Inc.,
Atlantic Highlands, New Jersey 07716 USA.

THE REORGANIZATION OF
SECONDARY EDUCATION

Dedication

To Pam, Emma and Luke

Contents

Foreword

This book is a most helpful contribution to our knowledge of the politics and public policy of secondary organization in Britain. It will be directly useful to many teachers and researchers of politics, public and social administration, and education not least, because it contributes to an art form that is all too rare in the academic enterprise. Too many scholars are concerned with pursuing new facts, an admirable activity in itself, without pausing to critically synthesize and reconceptualize what is already known. We can recall Daniel Bell's warning that research can be 'writing it all out in long hand'. Philip James has produced a scholarly essay which brings together all that is known on a subject that stands at the crossroads of many concerns: the reorganization of secondary education. His study rightly reflects the shift of political science from the more traditional studies of political institutions and the groups that work with them or against them and towards the study of the policy process.

The subject is ripe for this treatment. There is now a vast, but largely ignored and wasted, literature on the emergence of the comprehensive school in Britain. Much of it lurks in libraries as doctoral or masters' theses. Their authors, and those concerned with these issues, will be grateful for the way in which James has brought together the disparate developments in these key years of social policy. The profusion of the literature, indeed, reflects the importance and interest of the issues. More than any other issue (though perhaps the sale of council houses might draw even in some respects) comprehensive education marked the end of consensus in British local government, as well as in educational policy at large. For quite a long while the official policy of both parties assumed that a reasonable amount of equality could be induced through the offering of separate but equal kinds of secondary education in grammar, technical and modern schools. In particular, the endorsement of secondary modern education seemed to be a feature of a large number of local authority administrations of both main parties. The insistence on providing secondary education in a completely comprehensive system, and the opposition to this proposition, became a key issue in the 1960s and it still continues to be a dividing point in some local authorities. Policies have changed rapidly and drastically in response to the change in political fortunes both locally and centrally. It has entailed virtually the whole panoply of educational interests and the groups that represent them. Mr James well analyses both the ideology and the actions of the central government, local politicians, officials, teachers and parents. In doing so, he examines the relationships between these groups and their relative power positions in the policy making process. In doing so, he challenges common assumptions such as the dominance of central direction and initiative and the pervasiveness of CEO influence over decision making. He shows how the relationships are not static and how they vary among local authorities. The demonstration of how diverse patterns are between local authorities challenges easy generalizations and advances the cause of comparative studies.

This book also makes a stringent attempt to see what methods might apply in this field. Students of educational politics cannot eschew case study methods but it has proved difficult to accumulate knowledge systematically, let alone to develop theory, and James's essay is both critical of the particularity of some of the studies already written and helpful in discussing ways of creating the broader framework within which further studies can take place. Certainly, we need to derive what wisdom we can from the studies that we already have. Mr James identifies those areas where our knowledge is least, such as officer-member relations and the interaction between education and other departments, and where future research might most profitably be directed.

As this book is published, the main forces involved have again changed in their intentions and in their power relations. Yet new forces seem always to be on the horizon. Public opinion is not yet deeply affected by it but it is bombarded by a yellow press increasingly hostile to comprehensive education which puts strain on those who try to bring them into a stronger position within their communities. New social groups in Britain are emerging and simultaneously, some of the assumptions underlying the Taylor Report on the government of schools might cause a change in the structure of formal relationships.

So the patterns of the politics of comprehensive education will continue to engross general and specialist attention alike for some time to come. This essay will benefit all those who wants to engage themselves in these fascinating and complex issues.

Professor Maurice Kogan

Acknowledgements

This work began while I was a student at London University's Institute of Education and I would like to thank Dr D.A. Howell, Senior Lecturer in Educational Administration, for his help and encouragement. I owe a particular debt to the efforts of those who have undertaken the detailed case studies on which this work is so dependent.

Nearer home the unfailing cheerfulness and assistance of the library staff at the Dorset Institute of Higher Education have been greatly appreciated, and so have the equally unfailing patience and good humour of my wife.

Chapter One

Introduction

Traditionally the study of public administration has been very much concerned with the machinery and methods by which government policy has been implemented. More recently there has been a growing interest in the earlier stages of policy initiation and formulation. At the same time political scientists whose interests have often focussed on the study of voting, parties and pressure groups have developed an interest in the study of public policy making. None of this is totally new but the emphasis on treating policy as a central concept in both public administration and political science is a recent one. Parallel with these developments has been a renewed interest in the study of local government.

Much of the literature on local government in the past (and less excusably in the present also) has been characterized by an excessive legalism and institutionalism. Local authorities have been seen as no more than administrative arms of the central government. Wide generalizations have disguised the rich diversity between different authorities — a diversity which makes the study of local government such a potentially rich field for study. As Sharpe (1967, p.14) comments:

> The serious study of local politics is usually discounted for the not entirely surprising reason that it is too parochial. Paradoxically, it is perhaps in its broadening and enriching effect on our understanding of political activity in general that the study of local politics finds its greatest justification.

The traditional literature has tended to ignore the sources of policy initiative and formulation — a not' surprising result of seeing authorities more as administrative than policy making bodies. Consequently, although the literature gave fairly full accounts of the administrative workings ‾of local authorities we knew remarkably little about the nature of local party politics, relations with central government, the effects of local pressure groups and the interactions of members and officers as policy makers.

Policy making and administration within local authorities can only be fully understood as part of the political system of individual authorities and of the wider political system. As Stanyer (1976) has argued our understanding of local government is much enhanced once we appreciate the idea of local authorities as 'miniature political systems'. Each authority operates within a local environment comprising an electorate, organized pressure groups and parties and is also part of wider national political and economic systems. The authority can be viewed as an intermediary between the demands and constraints from outside its area and those from groups and individuals within its area including not least those from within the authority itself. In addition each authority has its own unique combination of social, economic and political characteristics, party system, political-administrative arrangements, values and traditions.

Educational Policy Making

Given the importance of education as a local authority function many of the studies of local policy making have chosen to focus on this area. This interest has been further encouraged by the growing recognition of the political nature of much educational decision making. The provision of education is almost completely a state monopoly and it is governments, central and local, which determine the priorities in terms of resources allotted to education as against other competing demands. In addition it is they who determine priorities within education as between, for example, different sectors of education. Such priorities reflect political judgements and are the result of a process of bargaining. In recent years such bargaining has become increasingly politicized as in the face of adverse economic and demographic factors the claims of education are increasingly challenged.

At the same time traditional boundaries as between central and local government, parents and teachers, education and other departments, have come under attack. Not only has there developed growing competition between different interests but also between competing values such as freedom of choice and equality of opportunity, accountability and independence, consumerism and professionalism. An era of consensus, expansion and innovation has been replaced by one of controversy, contraction and uncertainty about the future of education.

Secondary Reorganization

It is not altogether surprising that nearly all studies of educational policy making at the local level have been concerned with secondary reorganization. The issue has certainly been one of the most important in post war education. It has been one of the few educational issues which also became a major political issue. It aroused considerable feelings both within and between the rival political parties. It served to break the educational consensus between the Conservative and Labour parties. It caused major clashes between central and local authorities leading to a sharper drawing of party lines. It aroused more public interest than any other educational issue. It provoked considerable reaction from teachers both nationally and locally. It raised major ideological issues and as a policy it took up the time and energies of educational administrators for much of the last two decades.

The result is that secondary reorganization is now the best researched area of local policy making. Various studies have used it as a means of throwing light on such issues as the relations between central and local government, the role of political parties, the impact of local pressure groups and the relations between members and officers. The fact that the issue was interesting, topical and important in its own right served to disguise the question of how untypical it may have been as an example of local policy making.

Without exception the studies took the form of case studies of how individual local education authorities (LEAs) went comprehensive. In some instances two or more authorities were contrasted but in the main a single authority was the object of the exercise. Some of the studies were published but the majority of them remained in the form of unpublished dissertations. The net effect of this minor industry is that we now have detailed studies of the process of reorganization in a large number of English authorities — the interest has not spread to other parts of the kingdom.

The Literature

One of the earlier published studies was Saran's work (1973) on Middlesex. Unlike most of the studies hers looked at a number of educational decisions, including reorganization, over a period of several years. More typical was Batley *et al.* (1970) who studied the process of reorganization in two northern towns, Darlington and Gateshead. Pescheck and Brand (1966) also produced a comparative study of two towns, West Ham and Reading, but secondary reorganization was only one issue among others. The same applied to Parkinson's (1972) study of local education authorities (LEAs) in Merseyside. Fenwicke's work (1976 and 1980) has been mainly concerned with the process of reorganization as viewed from the perspective of central government but does refer to developments in a number of individual local education authorities (LEAs) as do Benn and Simon (1972). A brief study of reorganization in Croydon by Unwin has been published (Donnison *et al.* 1975). Even briefer studies include Northamptonshire (Eggleston, 1966), Norwich (Hewitson, 1969) and Brighton, Leeds, Brent, Havering, Hounslow and Newham (Peterson and Kantor, 1976). David (1977) refers to reorganization in a number of authorities but refrains from identifying them as does Jennings (1977).

In addition to such specific studies various writers have dealt with reorganization as part of a more general study of particular localities. Thus studies of Birmingham (Sutcliffe and Smith 1974, Newton 1976), London (Rhodes, 1972), Sheffield (Hampton, 1970) and Wolverhampton (Jones, 1969) all include references to reorganization in these towns.

The unpublished material consists mainly of dissertations for masters degrees with the occasional PhD dissertation. They are painstakingly detailed and collectively throw a considerable light on educational policy making. Despite this very little, if any, use has been made of them and the literature has been largely unexplored. They include studies of Bath and Southampton (White, 1974), Birmingham (Isaac-Henry, 1970), Bradford (Dark, 1967), Bristol (Wood, 1973), Croydon (Turnbull, 1969), Liverpool (Marmion, 1967), Manchester (Stern, 1971), Outer London Boroughs especially Merton (Lewin, 1968), Sheffield, Chesterfield, Doncaster and Rotherham (Fearn, 1977), Tynemouth (Eccles, 1971). All these studies deal exclusively with secondary reorganization. In addition the following unpublished studies examine this issue as part of a more general review of local policy making, Crawley (Rigby, 1975), Leicester (Mander, 1975), Oxford and Oxfordshire (Rhodes, 1974). Collectively the published and unpublished literature provides an enormous wealth of information on how various LEAs reacted to the challenge of secondary reorganization. The purpose of this particular study is to attempt to draw together the material and make such generalizations as seem appropriate. Generalization within the field of local government is fraught with difficulty as is doing justice to the peculiarities of the individual case studies. Nevertheless it is a task that should be attempted if the studies are not to remain isolated historical exercises. As Heclo (1974, p.x) has argued:

> One of the most crippling misconceptions in recent social science has been the presumption that original research consists solely in original data gathering. The result is a scholarly premium on writing new accounts and a dearth of cumulative studies trying to knit together what has already been learned.

In addition to examining the materials already referred to an attempt will be made to draw upon the wider literature relating to policy making within local authorities generally. Also, because it is believed that an understanding of local policy making requires an understanding of developments at national level an attempt is made to consider the more important changes at this level. It is hoped in trying to 'knit together' these various sources of material to provide a detailed account of how LEAs dealt with what was for them the major educational issue of recent years.

Plan of the Book

A number of writers have seen the main initiative for secondary reorganization stemming from central government rather than local authorities. Chapter Two therefore, considers the general issue of the relationship between central and local authorities and the controversial question of the degree of central direction. It traces the changing attitudes of central government and the various reactions of different LEAs and in doing so highlights the extent of their independence and the limitations on the powers of the central government.

Secondary reorganization evoked considerable interest and concern on the part of many parents and Chapter Three examines how and with what results they attempted to influence the course of events. It examines in particular the attitudes of LEAs towards parental involvement and the limits they placed on consultation. Reorganization also had major implications for the teaching profession. Chapter Four examines how over time the views of the various teacher unions changed and how local groups tried with varying success to encourage, discourage and modify the thinking of their particular authority. The relative power positions of teachers and parents are compared and an analysis is made of the factors influencing their degree of success.

Political parties are frequently seen as the major vehicle for policy change. Chapter Five examines the changing attitudes of the Conservative and Labour parties to secondary education and the factors influencing their policies. It then examines the ways in which local parties sought to control local decisions and considers the significance of party for this issue. Chapter Six is concerned with the respective roles of councillors and offices. It looks at the relationship between them and argues that the influence of officers may not have been as great as is often argued.

Although for purposes of presentation these various factors are treated separately they are intimately related to one another. Thus, for example, the nature and working of the party system will have major implications for the roles of officers and pressure groups within an authority. Some of these relationships are traced out in the concluding chapter. The main purpose of that chapter, however, is to consider in the light of these studies and the wider literature of public policy making the future shape of studies in the area of local policy. This is done partly by identifying possible substantive areas of research and partly by commenting on research methodologies. In this latter context, given the overwhelming predominance of the case study approach I consider its weaknesses and strengths and how it might most effectively be used.

Chapter Two

Views from the Top: The Influence of Central Government

A study of the role of central government is important for two reasons. Firstly, the central department clearly played an important role in the development of comprehensive education, though this role needs examination which will be attempted after dealing with the second reason. This is the viewpoint that central government so dominates local government decision making as to provide an almost complete explanation of policy at the local level. Thus Dearlove (1973) points to the dominant tradition in writing about British local government as one in which authorities are reduced to the level of agents of central government pursuing policies laid down centrally. Support for this argument usually rests on the growing dependence of local authorities on central finance and the existence of large numbers of central controls both of which are seen as producing uniformity in local services. Thus the Maud Committee (1967, p.76) commented 'We are clear there is a tendency for control and direction by central government to increase' — an opinion later shared by both Royal Commissions on Local Government (1969).

But there has developed in recent years a strong reaction against the view that local authorities are merely administrative appendages of central departments. (Alt, 1971, Ashford, 1974, Boaden, 1970, 1971, Boaden and Alford, 1969, Davies, 1968, 1969, 1971, 1972, Oliver and Stanyer, 1969). Part of the evidence for this counterattack consists of studies which show large variations between authorities in terms of expenditure patterns. The author of one such study has concluded (Boaden, 1971, p.20): 'The centre has a part to play in setting boundaries within which local authorities operate, but the divergencies within these boundaries must be explained elsewhere.' Boaden's own work suggests the explanation of such divergencies requires an analysis of local authorities as political systems in their own right. Within such systems he identifies three important dimensions affecting local policy making. The first of these consists of the needs of the area whether in terms of particular groups such as the young and the elderly or more generalized problems such as inadequate housing and community facilities. The second comprises the resources of the locality, including not only financial capacity but such other resources as manpower, organization, buildings and land. Finally, and linking the first two, the dispositions of members, officers and other important groups. These dispositions relating to such questions as what constitutes desirable standards of service, acceptable levels of taxation and legitimate areas of government involvement. It is these essentially local factors which are seen as crucial in explaining variations in services as between different local authorities.

Boaden's work is subject to certain limitations. His data relate to a limited period in time and to only one type of local authority, the county borough. As such it does not necessarily tell us much about the position in other types of authority or over longer periods of time. However, more recent work by Ashford (1974) has studied the effect of increasing central financing on both county boroughs and counties over the period 1949-67. His conclusion is that in neither case is there any evidence that the increase in central government funding lead to an equalization of the diversity of spending patterns of authorities. Such variations in the patterns of expenditure between authorities are hardly consistent with the suggestion of central control imposing strict uniformity of provision between them.

The freedom of local authorities to spend money as they determine is less dependent on the degree of central funding than on the nature of that funding. The extent to which local authorities are dependent on central government has probably been exaggerated (Crispin, 1976) and certainly varies considerably as between different areas. However, the important issue is less the scale of the support and more the extent to which authorities are free to spend it. A system of specific or earmarked grants would imply considerable central influence over how such monies should be spent. However since 1958 grants have increasingly been of a general or block nature. What this means is that although central government determines the total size of grant payable it has very little direct say over what local authorities choose to do with the money. Decisions as to what proportion of revenue to allocate to education as against other services are left to the discretion of individual authorities. They also determine the allocation of resources as between different educational priorities. Naturally there are constraints on the exercize of such discretion but there is very little the central government can do directly to determine how much grant money will be allocated to education or even more specifically to particular areas of education. The amount of grant an individual authority receives is determined by a formula which takes account of its relative wealth and demographic and social characteristics, but not the policies it chooses to pursue. Changes in the total grant payable to local authorities in general must, of course, have an effect on levels of expenditure. However, even here the individual authority is free to supplement a reduced grant by raising its revenue from the rates. This may be politically unpopular but remains a decision for the authority and not the central government.* If economies have to be made it is still up to the authority to determine just what these will be, even though the central government may offer suggestions.

Control over capital expenditure is tighter than over current expenditure. Before local authorities may borrow money to finance capital projects they generally require loan sanction from central government. The system enables central government to both limit the total capital expenditure of local authorities and to ration funds between different projects in accordance with their own sense of priorities.** Thus in 1966 local authorities were informed that loan sanction would only be given to secondary school building provided it was part of comprehensive reorganization. However, as can be seen

---

*Under the provisions of the 1980 Local Government Planning and Land Bill individual authorities which levy a rate poundage in excess of that laid down by central government risk a reduction in the grant payable to them. The intention being to pressurise individual authorities to keep their expenditure within centrally determined levels.

**At the same time the Bill provides greater freedom for authorities to determine their own priorities within the overall totals determined by *capital* expenditure.

from this example, loan sanction control is essentially negative. It may have prevented the building of new selective schools, it certainly could not force local authorities to close any existing schools or turn them into comprehensives. It would have little effect on authorities with sufficient secondary school accommodation while those less fortunate might decide to wait for a change of government!

This very inability of central government to determine the level of total local government expenditure has created growing concern on its part. This has been magnified by the rapid growth in that expenditure despite the relative stagnation of the economy. As a result a government committed to reducing the level of public expenditure generally is intending changing the basis of local finance in order to increase the degree of central direction. The extent to which they will succeed in doing so remains to be seen.

Departmental Powers
In much of the traditional literature there has been a tendency to list the various instruments of central control without any attempt to examine the extent of their actual use by departments, let alone the way in which local authorities respond to them. As a result central government's potential for control is confused with the actual extent and effect of control. The most comprehensive study (Griffith, 1966) of local-central relations available clearly shows government departments varying in their willingness to exert control, distinguishing between regulatory, laissez-faire and promotional roles. For example, the 1944 Education Act seems to give almost dictorial powers over LEAs. Professor Griffith (ibid) commenting on Section 1 of the Act which refers to LEAs acting under the Minister's 'control and direction' suggests this gives the impression of an unambiguous statement of a highly centralized system but that in practice Section 1 means less than it implies. Professor Kogan (1971) makes a similar point when he argues that the more detailed provisions of the Act place strong provisos against this almost dictatorial power of the Minister. This view is shared by such Ministers as Edward Short who has argued that Ministers' powers to interfere are extremely few and limited.

Other ex-Ministers, Boyle and Crosland, have also de-emphasized any overall controlling role (Kogan, ibid). The three Chief Education Officers interviewed by Kogan (1973) were very relaxed about central controls and didn't feel seriously inhibited by them. As Kogan summarizes, 'they see themselves within a national system of gently suggested guidelines rather than strong national prescriptions' (ibid, p.33). One of them, Dan Cook, makes the practical but often forgotten point that however powerful, compassionate and imaginative Ministers and senior civil servants might be it is difficult for them in education to take the initiative in the sense of getting things done. It would also appear that the Department is chary of using its wide powers of intervention for fear of damaging its relations with LEAs, on whose cooperation it is so heavily dependent.

That these powers are substantial can in no way be denied. They are particularly great as they relate to questions of structure and resources. Thus the Department of Education and Science (DES) is responsible for determining the ages between which children are minimally required to be in school, it projects the future need for teachers, it exercizes major controls over school and college building programmes, it negotiates with other departments the size of the grant payable to local authorities. In addition it has a general responsibility to ensure that educational provision is of adequate quantity and quality and that the rights of pupils, parents and teachers are safeguarded. It is required to ensure that such educational policy as is laid down in legislation and regulations is implemented in the localities. Further influence is exercized through circulars and memoranda and through the day to day work of Her Majesty's Inspectors. Specific sections of the 1944 Education Act give the Minister additional powers. Thus Section 13 requires an LEA intending to establish, cease to maintain or significantly change the nature of any school to obtain the Minister's approval.* Section 68 enables the Minister to intervene where he believes an LEA is acting or proposing to act unreasonably. Likewise Section 99 enables him to intervene where an LEA is failing to carry out its legal duties. All these sections have been used in connection with secondary reorganization. Conservative Ministers used Section 13 to save individual grammar schools from extinction and Labour Ministers to stop what they regarded as unsatisfactory reorganization schemes. Section 68 was used by Mrs Thatcher to force Surrey to retain selective school opportunities for certain children. Section 99 orders

---

*Although in 1979 there was some relaxation of these requirements the Secretary of State still reserves the right even where there are no local objections to call a proposal in and if necessary veto it.

have been made against named authorities for failing to proceed with reorganization as required under the 1976 Education Act.

At the same time it is important to note the limitations on DES powers. The 1944 Act lays the duty to provide education not on the Minister but on the LEAs. It is they who build and operate the schools and colleges and employ the teachers, who determine what proportion of their resources to devote to education and how to distribute it within education, who decide the pattern of secondary education within their localities. Thus much of the initiative lies with the LEAs themselves. It was they, not the Ministry, who pioneered the creation of comprehensive and middle schools and sixth form colleges. LEAs possess considerable political and administrative resources of their own and are prepared to use these to outmanoeuvre central direction where they feel it necessary.

DES interference has tended to be of a sporadic, discretionary nature rather than a continuous, tight control. Furthermore the DES itself is subject to various constraints exercised on it. In the same way as the LEAs are not agents of the Secretary of State but derive their powers from Parliament, so also does the Secretary of State. Thus his powers are limited by what Parliament chooses to give him and in the final analysis what the courts of law interprete Parliament as giving him. This point is well illustrated by the 'Tameside case'. In 1975 this Labour controlled authority made arrangements to reorganize its schools on comprehensive lines as from September 1976. When in May 1976 the Conservatives took control they determined to reintroduce selection for two hundred and forty places at two grammar schools. The Secretary of State acting under Section 68 of the 1944 Act directed the authority to revert to the 1975 scheme. Both the Court of Appeal and the House of Lords decided unanimously that in so doing the Secretary of State was acting unlawfully in that in the courts' opinion the LEA was not proposing to act unreasonably. This judgement served to show that the powers of the Minister were less far reaching than had previously been supposed and that his interpretation of what constituted unreasonable decisions need not go unchallenged.

Apart from such legal constraints there are also political constraints on the exercise of central power. The DES is not an autonomous department and like other departments is subject to Treasury, Cabinet and Parliamentary pressures. In addition it is subject to the influence of various groups not least the local authority associations and the teacher unions. The state of the economy, demographic factors, public attitudes and aspirations, party priorities and objectives, educational values and interests all affect the policy making options open to the department. Furthermore the DES is constrained by traditional respect for the idea of a partnership in educational policy making in which although it may claim to be the senior partner it has to take account of the opinions of its other partners and most importantly the LEAs.

Early Experiments

Turning now to the specific role of central government within secondary reorganization it should be noted at the outset that the 1944 Education Act did not lay down a tripartite system. It has been argued that this was the result of pressure from the Labour Party. Nevertheless, the two postwar Labour Ministers, Wilkinson and Tomlinson, broadly supported such a system as the norm. They permitted only limited experimentation with multilateral or bilateral schools and bolder schemes were discouraged. At the same time Fenwicke (1967) has pointed out that the significant factor about post war LEAs' plans for secondary education were that they represented considerable deviation from the Ministry model. While only two counties and three county boroughs intended to set up only comprehensive schools, nine and eleven respectively were planning at least one such school. Bilateral schools were even commoner. Fenwicke also argues that the fact the great majority of LEAs, including Labour controlled councils, opted for selective systems was less the outcome of pressure from the central government than the exigencies of sites, buildings and staff and the prevailing uncritical attitude towards selection.

This is probably a fair assessment of the situation but it would be wrong to suggest the Ministry put no pressure on LEAs wanting to introduce a comprehensive system. For example Saran's (1973) study shows that at this time two attempts by Middlesex to introduce comprehensive schools ran into Ministry opposition. The first in 1946 was referred back on the grounds that the proposed comprehensives were too small to facilitate viable sixth forms. At this point Labour lost control of the council and were not able to launch their second attempt until 1948. Their proposal to establish six such schools was initially pruned by the Ministry to two (later raised to three). In addition the Ministry set out criteria to be followed in choosing which two and these included teacher and parental approval, in effect giving these two groups a veto power over council policy. It also effectively prevented the proposed amalgamation of a grammar school and a secondary modern. The Ministry also informed them they would have to allow children within the catchment area of the comprehensive the right to take the 11+ and if successful opt for a grammar school, thus making it unlikely that the comprehensive would achieve a balanced intake. In 1952 Labour lost control and the Conservatives gained Ministry approval for a system of grammar and secondary moderns (apart from three comprehensives established by Labour). Although Labour regained power between 1958 and 1961 it was inhibited from attempting any major changes by the realization that the Ministry would not approve its ideas for abolishing the 11+ or the incorporation of existing grammar schools into comprehensive units. Thus Labour focussed its efforts on tinkering with the existing system by improving accommodation and equipment within secondary modern schools and making modifications to the selection procedures.

Certainly until 1965 both Labour and Conservative governments opposed any widespread introduction of comprehensive schools, focussing mainly on the difficulties associated with size and the threat they posed to existing grammar schools. Saran (Ibid, p.260) describes the role the Ministry played as 'advising, moderating, pleading, cautioning and ultimately wielding the big stick of refusing approval to any proposals which offended against national policy as interpreted by the Ministry'. Pedley (1963) is less charitable and describes the attitude of the Labour government as 'timid' and that of Conservative governments as 'stupidly obstructionist'. By 1951 after six years of Labour government only thirteen comprehensives had been built and after a further thirteen years of Conservative rule the number was still less than two hundred, around three per cent of all secondary schools.

Circular 10/65

The new Labour government elected in 1964 soon found itself under pressure from opponents of proposed schemes in a number of authorities and this led to a promise of a clear statement of government policy. On January 21 1965 the government moved the following Commons motion:

That this House, conscious of the needs to raise educational standards at all levels, and regretting that the realization of this objective is impeded by the separation of children into different types of secondary schools, notes with approval the efforts of local authorities to reorganize secondary education on comprehensive lines which will preserve all that is valuable in grammar school education for those children who now receive it and make it more available to other children; recognizes that the method and timing of such reorganization should vary to meet local needs; and believes that the time is now ripe, for a declaration of national policy.

This declaration came the following July in the form of Circular 10/65 which requested all LEAs to submit within one year plans for the reorganization of secondary education along comprehensive lines. However, as Professor Griffith (ibid) has commented the circular was a statement of national policy without the means to enforce it. The DES had no legal powers to force the submission of plans and even their submission and approval would have no legal effects. Nor did the circular incorporate any additional building programme allocation to stimulate reorganization. Of course, it remained true that if an LEA were to submit building plans which conflicted with comprehensive policy loan sanction could be refused and Circular 10/66 underlined this fact. But these levers depended on authorities taking the initiative and the DES being prepared to risk a situation of children without schools. The initiative remained firmly with the LEAs and the circulars were exercises in persuasion not compulsion. As one commentator on Circular 10/65 concluded (TES 18 March 1966): 'A diplomatic resistance, the skilful use of delaying tactics, a certain haziness in plans presented for the future are weapons which local authorities can use to effect . . .'. The Circular set no date by which schemes had to be started or completed. Several schemes which were submitted had no stated time scale, left out large areas or retained elements of selection. Some authorities failed to resubmit rejected schemes and others refused to make any submission at all (Corbett, 1970). As for Circular 10/66 this remained a wholly negative control for while it could prevent the building of new selective schools it could not of itself cause the closure of existing schools or the creation of new non selective schools.

Crosland (Kogan, 1971) has explained his decision to request rather than require the submission of plans in terms of his meeting with the Association of Education Committees and his assessment of the general mood of the local authority world. He must have been further encouraged by the fact that at that time most LEAs were Labour controlled and plans were in fact coming in at a rate the DES could only just cope with — 'The limitation was one of human and physical resources and not one of statutory powers' (ibid, p.191). Be that as it may, the situation changed drastically with the Conservative victories in the local elections of 1968 and 1969 and led the government to seek statutory powers, but being frustrated by inefficient whipping and electoral defeat. Assessment of the impact of 10/65 varies considerably. Benn and Simon (1972) criticize the approach as a mixture of political naivety and underpreparation by the Labour Party and DES assumptions that education could or should remain non-controversial. Nevertheless, the policy was far from unsuccessful and 10/65 was undoubtedly a major catalyst. Within five years of it the number of comprehensives rose from around two hundred to over a thousand. This still meant the vast majority of secondary school children were being educated in selective schools and the percentage in grammar schools hardly dropped at all.

Certainly the response to 10/65 varied according to which party controlled an LEA. Boaden and Alford (1969) found that whereas 54 per cent of Labour boroughs submitted plans within the time period only 32 per cent of other boroughs had. Heidenheimer and Parkinson (1975) found that by Labour's defeat in 1970, 115 LEAs had comprehensive plans either implemented or approved. Of these only 17 had had uninterrupted Conservative rule since 1966 and the great majority had been Labour controlled for the entire or significant parts of the period. All 16 LEAs whose plans were turned down had Conservative administrations for the bulk of the period. All 5 LEAs which submitted plans too late for the Labour government to evaluate them when it left office were Conservative. Seven of the ten LEAs who did not even reply to 10/65 were Conservative: the others having either no clear party system or a brief period of Labour rule.

The effects of 10/65 on individual LEAs obviously varied widely. In some it served to strengthen the position of those wishing to see selection abolished and by establishing a one year time-table for the submission of plans stimulated a sense of urgency into the process. This was the case, for example, in Tynemouth (Eccles, 1971) where schemes for non-selective education had for some time been attracting favourable attention and where 10/65 was awaited more with eagerness than apprehension. In other authorities the effect was very different. In Croydon (Donnison *et al.*, 1975) for example, where a comprehensive scheme was in process of being drawn up its effect was seen as making comprehensive education a clear party political issue and this led to the rejection of the scheme.

In authorities such as Bath (White, 1974) it seems unlikely that any moves towards comprehensive education would even have been attempted let alone succeeded but for the initiative presented by 10/65. Here the intervention of central government was very significant in stimulating fresh thinking in a situation where all the local parties had contributed to creating a selective system with an outstanding record of academic achievement and which had the full support of the Chief Education Officer and teachers alike. Similarly the majority Labour party in Southampton (White, ibid) was proud of that authority's selective system and did not seriously consider reorganization until 10/65 was issued. Again the Labour controlled Birmingham council (Isaac-Henry, 1970) had until 1965 not been sufficiently convinced of the merits of comprehensive education to even seriously consider dismantling their selective system. The decisive impetus in this case was therefore 10/65. Birmingham, the largest borough in the country and Labour controlled, was in a key position to set an example. It was left no alternative except that of taking issue with the Labour government and that was never contemplated. Thus, whereas in the March of 1965 the Labour Group had rejected a comprehensive proposal, by December it had itself produced just such a plan.

Undoubtedly 10/65 led to a situation where in many cases officials and members became involved in confidential discussions with DES officials in order to establish what would be acceptable to the Department. In this way central government was brought closely into the decision making process. Certain factors did serve to muffle the clash between the central and local authorities. Some LEAs had already gone comprehensive and their new purpose built schools showed the system working at its best. Many Chief Education Officers were becoming increasingly convinced of the system's merits. In rural areas the case was particularly strong and if this was less true of urban areas these were more likely to be Labour controlled any way. At the same time events did illustrate the ability and willingness of many LEAs to delay or refuse even to submit plans and the apparent inability of central government to overcome such opposition.

Into the Seventies

When the Conservatives returned to power attitudes to comprehensive education had hardened partly by the replacement of Boyle by Thatcher and because of the political necessity to support the newly Conservative LEAs which had been opposing Labour policy. Circular 10/70 withdrew both circulars 10/65 and 10/66. LEAs were informed that schemes need no longer follow comprehensive principles and instead '. . . educational considerations in general, local needs and wishes in particular and the wise use of resources' were to be the criteria. Schemes at present under consideration by the Department could now be withdrawn and new schemes need not be submitted.

Despite this, schemes for comprehensive reorganization continued to be submitted even from Conservative authorities. Many middle class parents were coming to see the 11+ as a threat to their children while some Conservative councils may have been more willing to submit schemes to a Conservative government since they could no longer be accused of compliance with the dictates of their political opponents. Also Labour was beginning to regain control of some LEAs. While Conservative policy was not to prohibit the building of comprehensive schools authorities were often prevented from incorporating grammar schools into their schemes. Between 1970–72 Mrs Thatcher used Section 13 of the 1944 Act to save nearly a hundred grammar schools and in 1970 made a rare use of Section 68 to force Surrey to retain selective school opportunities for children in areas chosen for the first stage of comprehensive reorganization. Also as part of a policy of giving priority to primary schooling, funds for secondary school building became more limited. Finally, approval was only given on a school by school basis whereas under Labour, schemes were approved as a whole. The intentions behind such changes may have been to slow down the rate of change but in the event the pace of reorganization was little altered.

On Labour's return to power Circular 4/74 was quickly issued requiring LEAs to submit reorganization plans by the end of 1974 if they had not already done so. Unlike 10/65 the circular was not only sent to LEAs but also to the managers and governors of voluntary aided and direct grant schools, illustrating the Governments determination to extend comprehensive education throughout the publically maintained sector. This was further reflected in the government decisions to abolish direct grant schools, threaten voluntary aided schools with loss of status and public funds if they resisted and LEAs with refusal of loan sanction for selective secondary school building programmes.

By the beginning of 1975 there were some two and a half million pupils in two and a half thousand comprehensive schools representing sixty-eight per cent of the secondary school population. In the previous ten years the number of grammar schools had fallen from 1,285 to 566. Of the LEAs in England and Wales 44 were totally comprehensives or had approval to reorganize. Of the remainder 60 were partially reorganized and retained selection for grammar school in some areas. Only one LEA, Kingston-upon-Thames, had no comprehensive school.

In August 1975 the government announced that for the first time special resources of £25m would be earmarked for comprehensive building programmes. In the following November, the government made clear its determination to deal with the seven LEAs who were openly refusing to reorganize and others who were dragging their feet or producing obviously unacceptable plans. At long last the government accepted that such remaining opposition could only be dealt with by statutory powers. As Regan (1977, p.53) concludes:

> Local education authorities of any political persuasion are disposed to follow a strong lead from the DES but where they feel unable to, even a determined Secretary of State has great difficulty in securing compliance. Despite the battery of financial and legal powers he possesses an adamant LEA is no mean opponent.

It was to deal with such LEAs that the government enacted the 1976 Education Act. This required those LEAs who had failed to submit satisfactory schemes to now do so within a specified time. In the event of submitted schemes being unsatisfactory the LEA could be required to resubmit. When such schemes were finally approved by the Secretary of State LEAs would be under a duty to implement them. Some twenty-nine LEAs were required to submit plans under this Act. These varied as between authorities such as Kingston which had resolutely refused to make any moves towards reorganization to those such as Essex where ninety-six per cent of children went to comprehensive school and where the conflict was limited to one particular area. The Act resulted in a series of court actions brought by both sides against the other and usually relating to the timing of schemes. Clearly some authorities were dragging their feet in the hope of a Conservative victory at the ensuing general election.

When this occurred the Tories lost little time in passing the 1979 Education Act which repealed those sections of the 1976 Act relating to comprehensive education. As a result LEAs have been able to withdraw proposals reluctantly submitted under the earlier Act and have returned to the situation experienced under the previous Conservative Government of being free to determine their own pattern of secondary education.

The Comprehensive Tide
Despite this the decade of the seventies has seen the trend to comprehensive education continue unabated. At the political level a number of factors have been important. First, the return nationally of the 1974–79 Labour Government which continued to press LEAs and eventually introduced legislation to force remaining authorities into line. Secondly, the success of the Labour party locally in recapturing seats lost in the late sixties. Thirdly, the reorganization of local authorities themselves meant that many areas retaining a selective system were brought under the control of educational authorities containing areas where selection had been abolished and the political difficulty of either reintroducing selection or allowing the survival of different systems within the same authority.

But in addition to such political factors the movement was encouraged by developments in public attitudes. The growing unpopularity of the 11+, the Achilles heel of the selective system, was buttressed by the findings of social scientists exposing the unfairness and arbitrariness of that system. Growing parental realization of the close relationship between educational opportunity and subsequent career chances produced unrest about a system where only a small minority of children received a grammar school education while the remainder were allocated to what many saw as inferior schools. Nor was the issue solely one of individual injustice but also of national inefficiency. Reports such as Crowther and Robbins showed evidence of reserves of untapped talent and stimulated concern about the resultant national wastage. This appeared particularly important at a time when Britain's economic performance compared to other countries was obviously disappointing. The comprehensive movement became part of the much wider movement to modernize traditional British institutions.

Clearly the role of central government varied according to which party held office. Apart from the immediate post war period Labour governments played an initiatory role first persuading and finally compelling LEAs to move in the direction of change. Conservative governments played a more adjudicatory role giving little positive encouragement to change and more concerned to judge the merits of proposals in the light of objections to them. Not that the role was that of an impartial adjudicator for the party clearly had its own views even though these changed over time. Given the largely negative nature of the controls central government can exercize over LEAs it is generally easier to stop changes than to initiate them. Thus it would, other things being equal, be easier for Conservative governments to prevent the abolition of grammar schools than for Labour governments to command the creation of comprehensives. Other things, however, were not equal and with the passage of time a ground swell in favour of ending selective education developed within LEAs as well as among many teachers and parents. Not only did this affect the thinking of Conservative governments but presented them with a situation where increasing numbers of LEAs, including Conservative controlled ones, were pressing them to approve reorganization plans. The result was the continued creation of additional comprehensive schools but often alongside selective schools. The Conservatives belief in the viability of such a mixed system, enabled them at one and the same time to appear apparently sympathetic to the need for reform and to still retain the basic elements of the old system.

By the end of the 70s, only fifty of England's ninety-seven LEAs still had any grammar schools left and only one authority, Kingston, had no comprehensives. The number of grammar schools had fallen by 1979 to two hundred and fifty three while the number of comprehensive schools had risen to well over three thousand. DES figures suggest that over eighty-three per cent of secondary school children now attent comprehensives compared with sixty per cent in 1974 and thirty per cent in 1970. At the same time such statistics need to be treated with caution. In many areas so-called comprehensive schools are effectively creamed of the top ten or even twenty per cent ability group by the coexistence alongside them of grammar schools.

In such situations it is difficult to see these comprehensives as much more than new style secondary moderns. A recent report (DES, 1979) by HM Inspectorate has shown that one in five of the comprehensives in their sample had no pupils from the brightest twenty per cent of the population and many of the remainder had none from the top ten per cent. Present plans to provide assisted places for bright children at independent fee paying schools would water down still further the comprehensive nature of many schools. So will government plans to enable LEAs to recruit children from neighbouring authorities sending the home authority the bill. This will mean that authorities with selective schools will be able to take children from surrounding comprehensive areas. It is the coexistence of selective schools which poses the greatest threat to the vitality and success of the comprehensive principle and which is logically inconsistent with that principle.

Chapter Three

Parent Power: Myth in the Making

It is often claimed that one of the special attributes of local government is its democratic nature brought about through the increased scope for extensive and informed public participation. For example, the Royal Commission of Local Government in England (1969, para.28) expressed the view that 'the importance of local government lies in the fact that it is the means by which people can provide services for themselves; can take an active and constructive part in the business of government; and can decide for themselves, within the limits of what national policies and local resources allow, what kind of services they want and what kind of environment they prefer'. Similarly, Dilys Hill (1974, p.15) has argued, 'Local authorities provide the essential ingredients of democratic society; elected representatives who are close to those they serve and who form an easy channel of communication between public opinion and the council'. Because of the more localized scale of government, members of the public are assumed to be more interested, informed and involved in decision making while councillors are better able to discern local feelings and needs. As one committee chairman caustically commented 'The real trouble with local government is that it is far too close to the electorate'. In particular, the system of regular elections is seen as contributing to popular control of local policy making.

Democracy at Work?
However, none of these factors necessarily imply anything about the relationship between the council and its electorate. The formal

decision making machinery may be seen by both sides as largely autonomous in operation and not particularly responsive to the attitudes and needs of the electorate. In such a system the council would be largely inward looking. On the other hand, councillors could be very concerned with the needs and reactions of the local electorate and highly responsive to their opinions. This, for example, seems to be the version of local government put forward by Jones (1969) in his study of Wolverhampton. Conceding the apathy of the majority — in all about 900 at most out of a population of 150,000 had an active interest in local politics — he interpretes this as reflecting their satisfaction. 'If things went wrong and services broke down, they would protest, agitate, organize and vote in strength. That they have never done so in Wolverhampton is a tribute to the responsiveness of the Council to the needs of the people of the town.' (Ibid, p.348).

It is often argued that the party system itself provides for the adequate consideration of local viewpoints including those of parents. Parties, it is maintained, have relatively open recruitment, are in competition with one another and articulate the expressed needs of local people. Others argue that the present party system is neither open nor competitive and that electoral control is tenuous. Electoral promises are necessarily vague and often overtaken by events. There is considerable evidence of public ignorance and apathy and not all commentators would follow Jones' interpretation of what this signifies. A study of Newcastle (Bealey *et al.* 1965) found that while four out of five voted in general elections only about two out of five did so in local elections and only one in four could name their ward councillors. Similarly Birch (1959) in his study of Glossop found very low rates of interest in local politics and a high degree of ignorance. Hampton's study of Sheffield (1970) showed that even where, as in that city, there was a close sense of community and attachment to the area this was often not connected with an interest in the politics of the area. Only four per cent of his sample were interested in taking part in local government, and twenty per cent could not name the controlling party. The opinion surveys conducted for the Maud Committee (1967) disclosed that twenty per cent of informants were unable to name a single service provided by their council and sixty per cent agreed their lack of knowledge of local government prevented them using their vote to the best advantage. In the light of this and other supporting evidence it would clear the air of a great deal of cant if instead of assuming that politics is a normal and common activity we made the contrary assumption that whatever lip service is paid to such an ideal, the reality is that for the great majority of people politics is alien and remote.

It has been further argued that councils themselves do little to dispel this remoteness. Keith-Lucas, (1961, p.9) for instance, suggests that local councils 'do not invite the people to think about such questions as slum clearance, and the development of schools, nor explain what the council hopes to do and the difficulties involved. In short, they do not treat the public as partners in the enterprise of improving or managing the town but rather as strangers'. This viewpoint is echoed in an observation of the Maud Report (1967, p.9) that:

> We have found no evidence to support the common belief that our local government has some uniquely democratic content. Whether the test is public interest, as exemplified by the percentage poll at elections, or the extent to which members of the public individually and in their associations are drawn into its processes, our local government does not appear to be especially democratic.

There is the view, nevertheless, that the electoral system still ensures councillor responsiveness to anticipated electoral reactions — the so called 'rule of anticipated reactions'. As a control mechanism this is almost wholly dependent on the accuracy of councillors' assessment of public opinion and their ascribing electoral importance to the implications of their own and their group's reactions. They may equally proceed on the alternative assumptions that the public remains largely ignorant of council decisions or have short memories or vote more on the record of national than local parties. Roy Gregory (1969) has carried out in Reading an attempt to test which of these viewpoints was commonest. Of the councillors he interviewed nearly all believed that the public's responses were fairly predictable and three quarters of them did not believe that if a mistake were made the public could be won over afterwards. On the other hand, most did not believe in the ability of the public to distinguish between the responsibilities and activities of central government and of the council or even to know which party controlled the council. When local election results in Reading were studied the fortunes of the political parties were seen to be very much in line with that of their national counterparts. From this it is difficult to conclude other than that national trends and policies have been significantly more important than local issues and policies in determining electoral results. The overwhelming impression from this and other studies (Sharpe, 1967) is that electors are quite ignorant of the basic facts of local political life and vote more on the basis of their orientation to national politics than to local events and personalities. Certainly Dearlove's (1973) study casts considerable doubt on the picture of local councils as weak in the face of public pressures and accordingly highly responsive to them. Rather, he shows how autonomous councils can be in the face of a largely passive and apathetic public. Boaden (1971, p.115) also argues 'It is possible that councillors trim their policy decisions to their expectations of popular reactions but our data suggests not very often'.

Other writers are less pessimistic. Newton (1976, p.19) for example, in a recent study of politics in Birmingham comments'There is no compelling reason for the law of anticipated reactions to operate in local elections and most councillors know this but nevertheless powerful forces push them to anticipate electoral reaction even though in their calmest and most logical moments they know their efforts have only a marginal effect' It may be, of course, that the greater sensitivity of Birmingham councillors is in fact a result of the large numbers of marginal seats in that town while the preponderence of safe seats in Kensington and Chelsea partly explains the greater autonomy of Dearlove's councillors. As always, there are problems in making any generalizations about local politics but the available evidence, some of which is discussed in Chapter Six, supports Dearlove's picture as being more typical than Newton's.

Furthermore, parents in particular are unlikely to mobilize their group power by voting as a bloc to bring pressure on their local authority. Rather they vote according to the usual divisions of class, sex and age. Thus parental power is dissipated and does not have the electoral effect that sheer numbers might suggest. Also given that education is only one element of local government it is difficult to see how there can be any specific expression of public opinion on educational policies as councillors are elected for their political views on a wide range of issues. The electoral command theory of politics has for a number of years come under increasing attack as unrealistic and nowhere more so than in local politics.

A Question of Attitudes

The fact is that there is only limited agreement about how far community involvement should go, about necessary levels of competence, about the exchange of information, the validity of local criticism and the degree and nature of accountability. There is certainly evidence that some politicians and officials oppose increased participation as unnecessary, expensive, time consuming and frustrating. Their reaction is often to restrict access to information and ignore reactions to information. What participation there is becomes a manipulative exercise in 'educating' the participants. 'Token' participation is no more than a means of legitimizing proposals already decided upon. Three interrelated stages are necessary if the public are to directly influence decision making: information, consultation and participation. Although a number of recent reports have called for improved communication between local authorities and the public, evidence suggests there is relatively little flow either way. Information access and control can be regarded as a power resource with councillors and officers acting as the information gatekeepers.

Professionals, whether teachers, councillors or administrators, have a natural tendency to maintain boundaries between themselves and 'non-professionals' in terms of participation in decision making. Officers may feel they are already accountable to elected members and see no need why they should be further accountable to other individuals and groups. In this context J. G. Davies (1972, p220) has made an interesting distinction between customers and clients. 'The customer is always right: he can choose, criticize and reject. The client, on the other hand, gives up these privileges and accepts the superior judgement of the professional. It is one of the aims of the would-be professions to convert its customers into clients and in so doing to stake out an exclusive area of discourse in which those trained in the skills and inducted into the mysteries of the trade can claim a monopoly of wisdom and proficiency'. Davies is talking specifically in his study about local authority planners and it may be that education officers have to date been less successful in staking out such a professional monopoly. Nevertheless, it is possible to discern in some of the comments of Chief Education Officers an implicit view that they know best what should be done. For example, the Chief Education Officers interviewed by Kogan (1973) all referred to the

increased parental interest in education linking it to the improved
education of parents themselves and their realization of the close link
between education and social mobility. Yet none of them saw
parental views affecting substantially the identification of what
needed to be done. Politicians equally may see demands for increased
community participation as a challenge to the decision making
prerogatives of elected representatives rather than the democratic
expression of local opinion. As Dilys Hill (1974, p.142) comments
'Central government accepts pressure groups as part of democratic
life. Local councils, by contrast, are more reluctant to encourage
what they see as an infringement on their right to govern'. Members
may also feel that increased public particpation merely confuses and
undermines confidence in the 'neutral' and 'independent' assessments
of the permanent officials.

Local government reorganization may have mixed effects on
participation. On the one hand local government has become more
remote with larger units and fewer councillors. On the other hand
there are more contested elections and increased party activity. Less
easy to assess are the effects, if any, on the attitudes of members and
officers to participation. If councils continue to feel there is no need
to improve local communication by consulting and working with
local people and groups and if officers remain suspicious and
sceptical about the need for participation the outlook must remain
bleak. As it is, popular participation is both a fact and a value. As a
value it rarely meets with open challenge; as a fact it rarely does more
than disappoint.

Parental Rights

The educational system itself is no exception to what has so far been
said and provides remarkably little by way of parental rights. Parents
are not, for instance, formally provided with the right to influence or
participate in the schools' curriculum or pedagogy both of which are
legally largely in the hands of the schools. The William Tyndale affair
illustrates the relative impotence of parents faced with teachers who
show almost total insensitivity to their concern about their children's
education and far from trying to gain the support of parents and
governors were contemptuous of them. Unlike some countries, no
British LEA makes it obligatory for a school to have a Parent
Teachers Association nor has any government seen fit to do more

than exhort their creation. Even where they are created they are in no sense decision making bodies. In the debate on the 1944 Education Act an amendment to insert a clause that at least one governor must be representative of parents was resisted by the Government. Even where parents are represented on such bodies it is doubtful whether they have much power and Baron and Howell (1974) have concluded that without initiative from the Head a governing body can do little to become an effective partner.

Whether the hope of the Taylor Report (1977) to increase parental influence through reforming the school governor system is likely to prove viable seems doubtful. Sheffield has been well in advance of most authorities in redesigning its system to allow greater parental representation on school boards. Nevertheless, a recent study has concluded (Bacon, 1978, p.135):

. . . this innovation simply gives an illusion of local participation in the decision making processes. This may well have the manifest effect of strengthening the public's confidence in the legitimacy of the policies being pursued within the schooling system. However, its latent, if unintended, function may well be to strengthen the position of those administrative-political elites ultimately responsible for the public's education.

Parent governors usually adopt the role these elites wish them to and this rarely extends to major issues of policy. Baron and Howell (1974) argue that governors have played a largely insignificant role in secondary reorganization. It is difficult to avoid the conclusion that governing bodies fall largely under the dual control of heads and local authorities and play a mainly marginal and symbolic role. The government's decision not to antagonize teacher and local authority opinion by increasing governors' powers as recommended by the Taylor Report is further evidence that this role is unlikely to change much in the future.

The specific provisions of the 1944 Education Act go only a little way in the direction of upholding parental rights. Section 76 seems to give parents rights regarding the choice of school but these are heavily constrained. As Lord Justice Denning stated in Watt v Kesteven County Council 'Section 76 does not say that pupils must in all cases be educated in accordance with the wishes of their parents. It only lays down a general principle to which the County Council must have regard. This leaves it open to the County Council to have regard to other things as well, and also to make exceptions to the general principle if it thinks fit to do so.' The court interpreted Section 76 as referring to the wishes of particular parents in respect of their own children rather than the wishes of parents generally which inevitably would be diverse and mutually incompatible. It was held that the Section referred to curriculum matters notably religious education and not the conditions of entry to a school. The court conceded that the parents had been presented with a fait accompli and that there had been hardly any consultation. However, it did not hold the authority at fault. Similarly an action by Ealing parents in 1967 claiming that the LEA had ignored Section 76 by introducing comprehensive education without sufficiently discovering parental opinion failed when the courts held it was impractical for an LEA to do this.

Section 13 required a local authority intending to close, establish or change the nature of a school to give public notice of its intentions and provides parents with a right of appeal to the Secretary of State. However the circumstances envisaged by the architects of the Act were where the initiative for change came from an LEA, with the Secretary of State acting as an impartial referee, and not the circumstances where the initiative came ultimately from the Secretary of State who in no sense could be regarded as impartial. Thus in the celebrated Enfield case the objecting parents were reduced to taking legal action over procedural points rather than obtaining an open-minded consideration of their objections from the Minister. It is difficult to see the case as in any way evidence for the existence of parental rights. In no sense was it upheld that parents had any right under the Act to a share in policy making but only to an observance of the procedure laid down in the Act. As one commentator (Buxton, 1970, p.212) has stated:

> The statutory framework of the education service nowhere gives any real right of control to the parents or to the ordinary citizen, and the courts have reinforced the wide discretion which this confers on the administrators by their refusal, even when the normal principles of statutory construction might arguably seem to allow it, to become involved in any question of policy or the merits of what is being proposed.

Parents have still been able to have some limited impact on

reorganization through pressure on the DES. As Minister, Mrs Thatcher was particularly attentive to local objections especially where well known grammar schools were involved. However, even Labour Ministers have not been deaf to local objections. Crosland, for example, after seeing a delegation of parents from Luton, opposed to the local plan, rejected it. The local Conservatives in this case had organized a petition of 11,000 signatures. Similarly Saran (1973) shows that Middlesex modified its 1948 scheme when grammar school parents protested strongly to the Ministry. Such protests also prevented, at a later stage, the abolition of the 11+ and the attempt to give a newly established comprehensive school a balanced intake. In general those parents who were actively involved were determined to defend the selective system and thus the status quo. The only exception of parental support for comprehensive education was in an area notable for its lack of a grammar school. And even here parental protest later developed when it was discovered that children in this area would not be allowed to attempt the 11+ and opt for grammar instead of comprehensive schooling. This protest led the authority to change their mind on this issue where admission to a particular school was desired on the basis of denomination, close family association or other valid reason. Parents were still not satisfied with this compromise and further protests led to that authority taking legal advice on parental rights regarding choice of school. This suggested that parents might well succeed in defending their right not to send their children to a particular comprehensive school. As a result of this advice and growing parental pressure, including a petition of over 3,000 signatures, the authority agreed that all children in the area of the comprehensive school would be permitted to take the 11+ if their parents so wished.

United We Stand — the Rise of Parent Pressure Groups

In attempting to bring influence to bear, both nationally and locally, parents have increasingly followed the lead of others in forming organized pressure groups. Stacey (1975) in her second study of Banbury found an increase in the number of specialist pressure groups linked to particular local authority services such as education. She sees this very much as a response of people to the increased scale and complexity of the decision making process. Many of these groups have only developed since the 1960's. The Confederation for the Advancement of State Education (CASE), for example, was founded in 1960 over what was a local problem and subsequently developed into a national organization though most of its 10,000 members are from the south of England. One of its aims has been to improve communications between LEAs and parents. It was, for example, after a meeting with CASE representatives that Crosland wrote into Circular 10/65 the request to LEAs to keep parents informed about their reorganization plans. A request also included in the Tory's subsequent Circular 10/70. As a national body its stance has been pro-comprehensive and this has been broadly true of its local associations with varying degrees of intensity. In Reading (Locke, 1974) the local group played a major role in pushing for comprehensive reorganization. In Croydon (Donnison *et al.* 1975, p.237) by contrast, the local branch examined the council's proposals but considered it 'inappropriate to express an opinion on the merits of the scheme'. In Banbury (Stacey, ibid) a local branch of CASE was created in direct response to the fears of middle-class parents' hearing of the county's plans to create a comprehensive school by amalgamation of local secondary modern schools with the Banbury grammar school. The association sent circulars to the Oxfordshire Education Committee, to the DES, and to local heads. Letters were also sent to individual members of the Education Committee and to local MPs. It also instigated discussions with the Chief Education Officer. Parish councils were contacted to bring their voice to the attention of the county. Even a research sub-committee was established to define the changing educational needs of the area and to examine alternative proposals. The members of the association came from those previously uninvolved in local politics. Their involvement now was largely as critical and informed consumers having between them considerable managerial talent. They were skilled in obtaining and using information and establishing links with any organizations likely to be helpful to them. They soon became a sophisticated and effective pressure group.

In general, local branches of CASE have exerted pressure in favour of comprehensive schools providing both a monitoring system and actively lobbying councillors and disseminating information which supports the comprehensive ideal. Not all parents have taken this stance. The National Education Association was formed in 1965 from those parents involved in trying to prevent the introduction of comprehensive schools in Enfield. Since then it has functioned to coordinate campaigns to save grammar schools in a number of areas notably Buckinghamshire and Surrey. A number of more localized groups also developed in the sixties both pro and anti-comprehensives such as STEP (Stop the Eleven Plus) and SOS (Save our Schools). Campaigns were often linked not only to LEAs' overall plans but also to individual schools.

Parent groups can be vocal on local issues as at Enfield and Ealing but are less able to press their case continuously as are the teacher groups. Apart from divisions of opinion between parents such groups generally lack the full time staff and the expertise of the teacher groups and to this extent are less effective in bringing pressure on local authorities. To the extent only a very small percentage of parents belong to such groups LEAs might challenge the extent to which they are representative. Parental attitudes towards reorganization seem not surprisingly linked to impressions of their own children's chances of passing the 11+. Given the relationship between this and social class there has been a tendency for middle class parents to be more defenders of selection than opponents. Nevertheless, growing numbers of such parents became increasingly aware of the risks involved and the arbitrariness of the process. Saran (Ibid) points out how in Middlesex officials conspired to keep from parents the facts of selection in that area fearing the wrath of parents in high ability zones who would have discovered how much harder it was for their children to win grammar school places. Even primary schools were prevented from publicizing their 11+ successes to prevent awkward questions being asked. But by the 1960's educational journalists and others were making it clear nationwide what the hidden implications and shortcoming of the selective system were and parents were not slow to alter their thinking in the light of such disclosures. Rigby (1975) in his study of Crawley refers to parental pressure being exerted upon the Education Department as a result of growing awareness of the stark contrast which existed between the grammar school with all its examination apparatus and the secondary modern schools which, at that time, had no external examinations.

Consultation — A Much Abused Term

One might assume that the comprehensive issue would be the sort of issue most likely to encourage public involvement in local policy making. It is worth noting, for example, that the study by Batley and associates (1970, p.2) is described in terms of being 'part of a study of participation in government in north east England' and that the comprehensive issue was specifically chosen as one 'that arouses deep concern and brings out into the streets people who normally show little interest in public life'. Yet neither in Darlington nor Gateshead was there any evidence of attempts to encourage participation and indeed on occasions decision makers seemed deliberately to discourage it. For example, in Gateshead the council seemed loath to risk exciting public interest which might have impeded the progress of its scheme. There was no real consultation with parents and the process of even informing them was very slow. They were not formally informed until after the scheme had received DES approval — 'it was felt that no information could be supplied until the plan was approved which effectively excluded the possibility of consultation' (ibid, p.93). Parents were regarded as not sufficiently informed to be consulted and lack of public response was taken to indicate either indifference or tacit approval. In the light of such attitude and the failure to provide information it was not surprising that the Education Office could report it had received not a single communication from parents on this issue. In Darlington parents were somewhat more involved due largely to the creation by a local teacher of a Parents' Action Committee to fight for reorganization and which in turn provoked the formation of a save the grammar school group. However, the general conclusion of this study is that 'The machinery of consultation seems, in both towns, to have been valuable as a pill sweetner. But it is hard to detect any point where the plans finally adopted were modified by the advice given' (ibid p.98).

A study (Peterson and Kantor, 1977, p.202) of reorganization in Brighton and Leeds and the four outer London Boroughs of Brent, Havering, Hounslow and Newham failed to find even attempts at the impression of public participation.

> Instead local councillors took special pains to keep information about their plans from becoming available to anyone except those admitted to an exclusive circle of decision makers. The teachers representatives who were consulted were pledged to secrecy. Neither the education committee meetings nor the various sub-committee meetings, where key decisions

were made, were open to the public. Announcements usually were not made to the press until the matter was brought before the borough council, at which point, the decision was a foregone conclusion.

Such public meetings as were held were to enable officers and members to tell parents what had been decided and only in one case, Havering, did they have any impact on plans. Cooption onto the education committee, apart from teacher representatives, was carefully limited to individuals with close partisan affiliations who could be relied upon to hold opinions similar to those of elected members. Such pressure groups as were formed were in large part front organizations for the political parties. Thus Havering branch of CASE was formed by prominent Labour leaders on the education committee while in Brent the major parent group was organized at a Conservative party meeting and partly financed by party funds. Jennings (1977) noted in the Outer London boroughs the ideological alignment between certain educational groups and one or other political party. However, he concluded that such alignments were not sufficient to impose much constraint on the parties who often saw other considerations as more important. Indeed, such groups were often seen by members as poorly informed and too strident in the presentation of their case whereas groups saw themselves as deliberately deprived of information and forced into abrasive tactics if only to stir up a largely apathetic public.

A study (Fearn, 1977) of reorganization in the Sheffield area found little evidence of parental influence. In Chesterfield, for example, the authority was suspicious that the more vocal parents represented the vested interest of particular schools rather than the wider body they claimed to represent. Such groups were seen as too ephemeral and dependent on one or two leading lights to merit much attention. In Rotherham where parental involvement was greater groups were mainly opposed to reorganization but given strong Labour party commitment could do little more than slow down the process. In Sheffield itself parental opinion was much reduced by the failure of parents to sink their differences even where these were fairly minor.

Of the four LEAs studied by Parkinson (1972) only in one, Liverpool, did the comprehensive issue attract public attention. In the other three towns no groups at all emerged either supporting or opposing apart from ad hoc groups relating to particular schools.

White (1974) found in Southampton the wider community remained mainly apathetic, uninvolved and unconcerned. The only exception to this was the local CASE group which was pro-comprehensive. A similar picture emerges in the study by Pescheck and Brand (1966) where again the recipients of the educational service are seen as apathetic with neither officials nor members appearing to make any efforts to dispel this apathy. In West Ham Pescheck makes the point of the possible connection between the absence of a middle-class element and the absence of any organized parent groups. Other studies have also found a relationship between class and organizational membership.

Isaac-Henry (1970) found that in Birmingham parents were never effectively organized over this issue. The only group purporting to represent parents was the local branch of CASE which had about 150 members. It is not even clear that the branch wanted to play a part in consultations and in any case its membership was almost wholly divided over the question of reorganization. As far as the LEA's role was concerned what meetings there were with the public were used more as a means of explaining plans than for consultation. Such meetings were also held after final decisions had already been taken. Lewin's study (1968) of reorganization in the outer London boroughs distinguishes between three patterns of consultation. A committee decision followed by advice from the public; the public being encouraged to initiate proposals or comment on a number of possible schemes; a compromise arrangement where the committee makes a limited decision and then asks for public reaction. Lewin found no evidence to suggest that any one pattern produced happier results. Means of consultation varied. Public meetings were commonly used but the numbers of such meetings ranged from over a hundred in Waltham Forest down to three at Havering and Richmond and only one at Redbridge. Only two authorities, Harrow and Richmond, consulted Parent Teachers Associations and only three, Kingston, Richmond and Sutton consulted local CASE branches. There were sharp variations in the amounts of information provided and, in Lewin's opinion, few LEAs found the happy medium between too much and too little. While they were generally willing to keep the public informed of their plans they were less willing to provide actual opportunities for the submission of views before decisions were reached. The general impression, apart from Enfield, was of the absence of expressed public opinion and acquiescence from local parents. Thus Lewin's final comment is that 'the art of successful educational administration of major policies may hinge on pulling the public dragon's teeth by asking for its views — especially as the mass of people don't have any'.

Some Success Stories

In just a few LEAs parents have been more influential than this statement might imply. Reference has already been made to the impact of parental opinion in Middlesex (Saran, ibid). Parkinson (1972) found parental involvement in Liverpool of some importance and this is supported by Marmion's study (1967) of that city. Here the most active and successful group was the Liverpool Parents Protest Committee campaigning against reorganization. This was established following Labour's decision to reorganize in 1963. Most of its support came from parents of grammar school children but also parents of secondary modern school children whose schools were programmed for integration with notoriously tough schools or in the case of girls where the scheme was coeducational. The group appealed for education to be taken out of politics and on this basis approached the local Labour party only to be rebuffed. From this point on the main efforts were aimed at collecting signatures for an appeal under Section 13 of the 1944 Act to the Minister. In this they were successful in collecting 32,000 signatures. The reasons for this strategy being the realization that the controlling Labour Party saw the group as representing a relatively small sectional interest and that it was an interest they were determined to ignore. Nor were other groups, such as teachers, willing to align themselves with a group which was engaged in such a bitter quarrel with the authority. Therefore, the group turned its attention to central government and tried to establish its credibility there by demonstrating wide public support through its petition. Although probably not decisive in causing the Secretary of State in 1965 to reject half the Liverpool scheme the very large numbers of signatures may have influenced the Minister as a possible electoral threat. The important point, however, is that the group was quite unable to succeed in exerting pressure directly on the LEA and whatever success it may have achieved was brought about indirectly.

In Sheffield, Hampton (1970) discovered that parental opinion was not mobilized until 1965 and then largely by parents of grammer school children concerned to protect their children's schools. This

sparked off a counter group originating with two of the staff of
Sheffield University who brought new life to the nearly moribund
local branch of CASE. However, the degree of public interest
aroused was never great and plans for reorganization were quickly
drawn up in 1965 and given DES approval the following year.
Nevertheless, both parties were throughout very aware of the large
numbers of parents who opposed selection and this encouraged
moves towards reorganization and inhibited a reversal even when the
Conservatives took control in 1968.

In Bath, (White, 1974) there was a remarkable degree of
involvement in the early preparation of plans. This is attributed to the
personal attitude of the Chief Education Officer and the established
tradition in the town of informed and involved public discussion of
locally controversial issues. This question of tradition and local styles
of government is important as in other LEAs there is an equally
strong tradition of avoiding such public discussion. In Bath the
resultant public opposition caused the Council to reject proposals for
reorganization — a process described by a local Labour education
spokesman as 'death by consultation'. However, later a growing
degree of political decisiveness and authority was able to override
such objections and the selectivists were not able to use again the
consultative process to gather their forces and defeat proposals. Also
there was evidence that if the process of deciding on plans goes on too
long the public tend to become confused and gradually indifferent to
the final outcome.

Obstacle to Parent Power

An LEA considering reorganization may not be wise to exclude
general public opinion from its calculations and indeed Circular
10/65 specifically required it to take account of such opinion. Groups
in favour of reorganization might be harnessed to advantage while
the existence of counter groups whose efforts might hinder and
disrupt reorganization cannot be wholly ignored. Public knowledge
of reorganization may be minimal or misinformed and the LEA
could attempt to allay fears and remove misconceptions. Secrecy can
equally arouse resentment and suspicion and encourage rumours.
Yet involving the public also poses problems. In particular it raises
problems of how, when and for what purposes consultation is being
used. The one way communication of information is much easier
and not surprisingly this is the furthest many LEAs went. Failing to

arouse interest it was all too easy to then interpret the ensuing silence as representing general consent. Furthermore, parents were never a unified group on this issue and it would be wrong to see the relationship as one between the LEA and the public. There were many publics with different views and to the extent attention was paid to these, LEAs were in the business of reconciliation and arbitration. Parents never had the role of initiating proposals but only of responding to the proposals created by others. As Fenwicke (1967) concludes 'Policy initiatives are seen to be prerogatives of the LEA'. This is in line with Hill's (1974) suggestion that in local government the dominant tradition is one of telling citizens about decisions which have been largely decided upon rather than enouraging interested people to contribute to the making of policy.

The attitudes of members and chief education officers to the release of information and the obligation to consult varied considerably. Also some groups were given greater respect than others. Dearlove (1973) has drawn attention to the selective perception of local authorities in relation to local pressure groups. His study suggests that councillors assessed group claims by categorizing the source of the claim, the claim itself and the means by which the claim was made. Generally speaking, the groups councillors were sympathetic to either those seen as assisting the council in the provision of some service or presenting demands which did not challenge established council commitments. Groups which were seen as unhelpful tended to be ignored as legitimate sources of information or opinion. The sources that were most looked to were those most likely to provide information and opinions supportive of councillors' own views rather than those that might give rise to challenges to those views. Councillors may well see the independent articulation of local opinion as a threat to their claim to be local representatives and spokesmen. Consultation represents a challenge to party domination and makes decision making less autonomous and predictable. Likewise officials may see consultation as a threat to their claim to be professionally objective and detached from outside pressures. Sharpe (1973) has described the system as one of 'obsessional professionalism' whereby the public interest is viewed less as the outcome of opposing group pressures but rather as 'the right way' to tackle particular problems.

To the extent councillors were unsure of likely parental responses to reorganization, the safest policy would be to minimize opportunities for such responses to be effective. Thus a number of authorities provided a minimum of information and did little to actively encourage consultation. Where parent groups did develop, LEAs were often able to play off one against another and write them off as unrepresentative. Where there is majority rule and a political will for change groups opposed to such change are particularly disadvantaged. Parents were not considered as strategically important as teachers were nor as having the expertise of teachers in educational matters. Their greater numbers and potential electoral power rarely became a reality given the nature of the local electoral system. They were further disadvantaged by the relative absence of machinery for regular consultation. This, of course, no more than reflected their major disadvantage, the absence of a tradition, in either education or local government, of meaningful consultation with client groups.

Chapter Four

The Professionals: Teacher Tactics

In what we may term the central government of education teachers undoubtedly play a major role alongside the central government and the local authority associations. As Manzer (1970, p.1) comments 'Most decisions about national educational policy are made within a tripartite structure involving the Department of Education and Science, Local Education Authorities and organized teachers'. These teacher organizations are formally recognized interest groups and consulted over a wide range of educational issues affecting their membership including teacher supply, salaries and conditions of work, the raising of the school leaving age and comprehensive reorganization. They present their views through lobbying, publicity, deputations, membership of committees, Parliament and perhaps most importantly through regular contacts with officials. As Manzer comments educational pressure groups must convince the civil service and this is best done through private consultations rather than ritualistic deputations. Apart from regular departmental consultations it has been common practice to invite them to give evidence to the various committees of inquiry into education. In this way their views have usually influenced official thinking on education whether it be questions of style, content or organization. It is also standard practice for the Department of Education and Science to send them drafts of proposed circulars for comment. It was the National Union of Teachers' comments on the draft of Circular 10/65 which persuaded Crosland of the need to persuade LEAs to consult teachers over reorganization.

The three main teacher unions, the National Union of Teachers (NUT), the National Association of Schoolmasters (NAS) and the Joint Four, have a combined membership of nearly half a million. The National Union of Teachers (NUT) is by far the largest and most powerful of the three. Coates (1972) has pointed out that three out of four teachers belong to one of these major unions and that teachers are among the most highly organized of all worker groups.

The Unions not only operate at central level but also maintain a system of local branches. Thus the National Union of Teachers (NUT) has a network of such branches which broadly correspond with the areas of LEAs and can negotiate directly with them. It is through such branches, for example, that teachers are selected for cooption onto local education committees. It is also through branches that the unions keep in touch with developments at local authority level and this can result in pressure being brought to bear on individual authorities. Many LEAs have teachers' consultative committees. The Chief Education Officers interviewed by Kogan (1973) all paid lip service to involving teachers in the decision making process. For example, one of them, Dan Cook commented 'I believe that it is right that teachers should have a powerful influence on decision making and a good authority takes teachers into its confidence . . . It is important that the teachers should be seen in the education office, as for example, members of working parties and playing their part in policy discussions' (Ibid, p.91). It could thus be argued that at local level there is something like a comparable triumvirate to that described by Manzer at central level — a triumvirate of members, officers and teachers.

The Teacher Unions

The stances taken over education issues have varied over time and by union. Thus in order to form a balanced judgement of the role of teachers requires paying some attention to the evolution of their views throughout the postwar period. Fenwicke (1976) makes the point that in the early 1940's most of the teacher groups expressed a widespread if short lived enthusiasm for the multi-lateral school.' This is supported by Dr Gosden (1976, p.303) who comments 'The Joint Four pressed quite strongly the argument in favour of multi-lateral schools . . . and there was considerable agreement among teacher organization generally on the merits of these schools*. That this common attitude soon broke down is evident in the events surrounding Middlesex's attempt (Saran, 1973) to reorganize. Here the local branch of the NUT expressed commitment to the comprehensive principle while it was consistently opposed by the local branch of the Joint Four. This became increasingly the pattern as teacher groups response to reorganization became more and more sectional reflecting the traditional divisions within English education. On the one hand were the groups such as the Joint Four representing largely teachers from selective schools and on the other hand the NUT and the National Association of Schoolmasters (NAS) much more representative of teachers generally and recruiting mainly from primary and secondary modern schools.

Kogan (1975) has argued that the NUT has generally advanced views in keeping with liberal progressive assumptions. For example, arguing for informality in teaching methods, flexibility in examination arrangements and the elimination of artificial barriers between different stages of education or types of secondary school. In its attitude to comprehensive education it has had to take account of the views of its own grammar school members. Within the union there has been a strong committee of grammar school teachers firmly committed to preserving the selective system. The union also, to some extent, has supported the view that if secondary modern schools developed GCE streams parity of esteem could become a reality. The National Association of Schoolmasters (NAS) at their 1954 Conference passed unanimously a resolution to the effect that there was not yet sufficient evidence to justify the widespread establishment of comprehensive schools. The Assistant Masters Association (AMA) was passing similar resolutions and also hostile was the Incorporated Association of Headmasters which reaffirmed its opposition throughout the 1950s. The President of the latter speaking of 'false egalitarianism' and 'the heresy of grammar school education for all'. The Joint Four's response to Labour's 1953 'Challenge to Britain' was to deplore the idea of building large numbers of comprehensives and in the process devaluing well-

---

*In the 1940s the term multilateral implied a secondary school catering for all children in a given area but within clearly defined sides or streams. Thus within the school organization, grammar, technical and modern divisions would retain their distinctive character.

established grammar schools. Even the NUT at its 1954 Conference opposed further comprehensive experiments until the existing ones were proved satisfactory. In the run up to the 1955 general election the NUT stressed the need to protect the freedom of LEAs to determine their own forms of secondary education.

By the late 1950's there was growing teacher realization of the anomalies of the selective system and the growing challenge of the comprehensive alternative. In 1957 the NUT produced a symposium in which heads of comprehensive schools described the work of their schools giving a most encouraging picture. In 1960 the NUT's first executive member teaching in a comprehensive school was elected. At around this time the AMA's attitude to comprehensives began to unfreeze partly in response to the increasing numbers of its own members working in such schools. As the numbers of such teachers grew it became increasingly unwise for teacher unions to appear totally unsympathetic to such forms of school. The NUT actually used many such statements as part of a strategy of attracting comprehensive teachers away from other unions. Also a major problem arose for local branches in areas where reorganization was being actively considered. There was the fear that if their national association's stance was too dogmatic and inflexible local branches might not even be consulted. For many, reorganization by the late 1950s and early 1960s was not merely an academic debating issue but a very real possibility. Earlier reactions of approval or disapproval now required translating into acceptance of change and attempts to modify policies. By 1964, the NUT was cooperating with the Joint Four in producing a common statement which was concerned with procedures for consultation and protecting teachers' professional interests and not with arguing the case for or against reorganization. The Joint Four while continuing to make a strong plea for the grammar school was obliged to leave the door open for change. Groups such as this, faced with a committed central government could do little more than focus their energies on procedures for planning and implementing change. Their tactics were to examine each proposal carefully to safeguard the interests of the more academic child as well, of course, as those of their own members.

By 1965 the NUT was giving evidence to the Plowden Committee favouring the abolition of selection. This was the first time the union came out so clearly in favour of comprehensive education on more than a purely experimental basis. There is little doubt that this must have encouraged the Labour Party to have come out strongly in favour of reorganization the same year. Over the next few years the NUT officially supported government policy arguing for tougher measures of enforcement. For example, in 1969 a resolution was passed at the Annual Conference calling on the government to make the necessary legislative changes to bring about comprehensive education by abolishing selection for secondary education. Apart from arguments relating to the unfairness to pupils of the selective system many NUT members as secondary modern teachers themselves felt disadvantaged by the system. Not only had they the most 'difficult' children to teach but they lost their best pupils to the grammar schools. Not only did they feel their schools lacked parity of esteem but also parity of resources with grammar schools. This they felt resulted also in poorer career prospects compared with their more favoured and esteemed grammar school colleagues.

Teachers were active within the Labour Party nationally through the National Association of Labour Teachers (NALT). As early as the 1946 Party Conference the Association urged on the then Minister, Ellen Wilkinson, the need to reshape the educational system in accordance with socialist principles which they interpreted as meaning multilateral reorganization. Despite general Conference support for the motion the Minister was not persuaded. In subsequent years and Conferences NALT continued its barrage of criticism of party policy. This reached a peak when the new Minister, George Tomlinson, rejected the Middlesex plan for reorganization. The Association attacked him for defending the tripartite system as 'usual and logical' despite the views of his own Party's Conference. When in the 1950s the Party published its proposals for comprehensive education in its policy document 'Learning to Live' NALT was quick to criticize. It attacked the suggestion of a split system of junior and senior comprehensives as unnecessarily divisive. As a result of this criticism the document was redrafted on the basis of the NALT amendment calling for all age, orthodox comprehensive schools. When on their return to office the Party came to consider the question of implementation NALT argued strongly for legislation to enforce reorganization. In this way they ran into substantial opposition from those members of the party who had a higher regard for the autonomy of LEAs and the party avoided an explicit declaration of a policy of legislation. NALT also, at this time, offered its services to any LEA wanting further information about comprehensive systems. These Labour teachers undoubtedly kept the case for comprehensive school alive despite the response of the party both in and out of office and the fact that for the majority of Labour MPs secondary education was never an issue of any great interest.

The Conservative teachers association had taken a hostile attitude towards multilateral schools after the war and their function of supplying information to the Conservatives' education group in Parliament probably contributed to that body's hardening attitude towards the issue. As Fenwicke (1976, p.80) has commented, 'Throughout this period the Conservative teachers assocation was the backbone of support for tripartism and opposition to the "triumph of mediocrity"'. Although they accepted certain criticisms of the 11+ as valid they could see no alternative to selection in one form or another.

Teacher Consultation

When the Labour government finally committed itself to reorganization it was careful to take account nationally of teacher opinion. In the same way it desired that Local Education Authorities should likewise take account of opinion from local teachers. Thus Circular 10/65 required them to consult with teachers and it is difficult to envisage any Local Education Authority proceeding with such a major change without such consultations. As one Deputy Chief Education Officer has commented '... the education officer will always have in the forefront of his mind that a scheme with the backing of the teachers' associations is more likely to work than one that is opposed. Conversely, he will advise his committee to think twice about any scheme that all the teachers' associations condemn' (Birley, 1970, p.98).

Nevertheless attitudes towards the value of teacher consultation vary as between different Chief Education Officers. David (1977) on the basis of research involving large numbers of senior education officers distinguished betwen two styles of administrator which she terms 'educators' and 'conciliators'. Such differences, deriving in large part from individual personalities, were found to relate to attitudes regarding both teacher and parental consultation. Those CEO's defined as 'educators' saw their task as making professional educational proposals legitimate and saw consultation with teachers as fellow professionals an important part of their function. At the same time they were less likely to include parents as legitimate educational interests and saw only the need to inform them of decisions. 'Conciliators' saw their role in terms of arbitrating between different interests and accordingly the need to involve both parent and teacher groups. Seeing their role more in administrative and political than educational terms they were less likely to distinguish between the two groups in the sense of seeing teachers as a more legitimate professional interest.

Turnbull (1969) in his study of Croydon found that the degree of consultation varied over time not least depending on the character of the particular Chief Education Officer. In the 1940s and the early 50s the Chief Education Officers' attitude to consultation was that it meant calling heads to the office to tell them what the latest policy was. Initially only heads were consulted — the Secretary of the Croydon Head Teachers Association having made a special point of cultivating a relationship with the Chief Education Officer. Later a Joint Consultative Committee was created consisting of three teachers elected for the quite impossible task of representing primary, secondary and further education. This largely ineffective body served as an excuse to prevent the establishment of more effective machinery. The next Chief Education Officer, Wearing King, had previously been the Deputy Chief Education Officer and had almost inevitably been influenced by his predecessor's attitudes. Thus his early attempt to introduce a Sixth Form college was characterized by an almost complete absence of consultation and indeed, as pointed out, little real machinery existed for this. His next attempt, in 1961, was also characterized by minimal consultation limited to four head teachers only and no attempt was made to consult rank and file teachers. By the mid 1960s attitudes to consultation were changing as a result of two factors. First King resigned and was replaced by his deputy whose attitude towards teacher involvement was much more positive. Secondly, as a result of London local government reorganization Croydon absorbed Coulsdon and Purley. Croydon teachers had been campaigning for some years for improved consultation but were now joined by teachers who had been accustomed to regular consultation. Also the Council now included new members from these areas who also were used to and sympathetic towards teacher involvement. As a result, for the first time Croydon teachers were allowed to sit on the Education Committee and its subcommittees. From the mid 1960s they were strongly represented on all working parties and it would appear that increasing attention was given to their attitudes both by members and officers though Turnbull is cautious in claiming that they had much actual impact on events which seemed more determined by party political considerations.

In Middlesex Saran (1973) found that the Chief Education Officer took the view that secrecy had to be maintained until a policy was settled while the Education Committee went still further and felt that staff should not be informed until the Ministry had given approval. The result was that many assistant teachers first heard of possible reorganization through press advertisements and news of letters of dismissal sent to heads. What prior consultations there had been were limited to head teachers. Not surprisingly teachers complained bitterly at this lack of consultation including teachers who supported the comprehensive idea. The attitude of the authority appears largely unrepentent. Indeed, the Chairman of the Education Committee, strongly criticized one head for speaking out against the policy of his employer. The head was subsequently severely disciplined by the Chief Education Officer and would have lost his job but for the intervention of the NUT. More generally, the handling of the issue by the LEA had made all teachers feel insecure and this increased hostility to change. It remained true to say that at that time, the late 1940s, very few teachers had more than the haziest idea of what a comprehensive school was like. Thus there was an obvious need for the LEA to take the initiative in explaining and persuading the teachers of the merits of such schools but this they failed to do. Teachers' fears about security would not have arisen had the LEA taken more seriously the need for consultation instead of assuming that policy decisions were the preserve of the council and that teachers neither would nor should oppose such decisions. Councillors were further encouraged to adopt these assumptions by officers and it must have come as a blow to both when the Ministry required that schools selected for reorganization would have to be in areas where both teachers and parents where sympathetic to change. In this situation the attitudes of parents and teachers were crucial in determining whether reorganization of a particular school proceeded or not. Thus one scheme involving turning a grammar school into a comprehensive school aroused a general outcry from grammar school teachers seeing this as the thin edge of the wedge. The teachers capitalized on the failure of the LEA to inform and persuade parents by holding their own meetings with parents and putting strongly and effectively the case for preserving the grammar school. This led directly to the formation of a parents committee and joint teacher and parent protests to the Ministry and the LEA. When the Education Committee did get round to addressing parent meetings it found itself faced with largely hostile and informed groups. In the light of this situation, largely of its own making, the authority abandoned its proposals.

The value of consultation from the LEA's point of view is illustrated by the case of Tynemouth (Eccles, 1971). Here teachers were generally doubtful about reorganization and unanimous in favouring the retention of selection. They admitted it produced injustices but proposed dealing with these by providing additional places at selective schools. The Joint Four attempted to justify selection as being in the interests of all children. 'It is generally accepted that for the benefit of all children they must be graded into groups of similar ability. This is not a privilege given to only able children but enables all children to make progress at approximately their own pace in accord with their aptitude' (Eccles, 1974, p.38). Other teacher groups feared that comprehensive schools would lead to a lowering of standards and a sacrifice of the interests of the able child. Some secondary modern heads reacted against the proposal seeing their efforts to build up their school threatened by dismantling them. The very fact that children in non-selective schools were successfully completing O-level courses was not interpreted as pointing to the natural evolution of a comprehensive system so much as evidence of the flexibility of the selective system. Opposition increased following Circular 10/65 as teachers claimed none of its schemes were practical given existing buildings and DES failure to provide special funds for reorganization. The local Head Teachers Association deplored 'the imposition of comprehensive education'; the NAS asserted the present system 'is the one which has worked as well as any system devised by man can work' and even the NUT felt the time was 'not yet right for reorganization'.

Yet the readiness of the LEA to seek teacher opinion undoubtedly influenced the teachers' decision to opt for constructive cooperation rather than obstructionism. 'By keeping teachers informed of its own thinking on possible policy development; by inviting their observations; by emphasizing that they would have a real contribution to make at the detailed planning stage, the authority managed, to pre-empt too hostile a reaction and laid the foundations for a partnership that was to carry through the change.' The LEA accepted that a fundamental reshaping of secondary education without involving teachers was both undesirable, since planning would lack the benefit of their experience and dangerous since bitterness might result.

The Education Committee had established a Second Schools Committee which in turn created a working party of eight head teachers, eight assistant teachers and seven members of the Education Committee. Each secondary school and each teacher organization was represented and as a teacher dominated body it acted as an effective sounding board for teacher opinion. The working party established additional sub-committees which were also teacher dominated and included teachers not in the working party. Thus teachers had ample opportunity to make their views clear to the LEA. The working party's function was to make recommendations on the means by which policy decisions taken by the LEA could be translated into effective plans. It is important to note that the committee was only established *after* the council had approved the proposal to go comprehensive.

Nevertheless the teachers were effective in settling details of reorganization. For example, on an important vote in the working party on coeducational or single sex schools the seven education committee members all abstained having presumably decided this was a matter best left to the teachers — even though these were divided nine to five and the education committee members vote could therefore, have been decisive. Teachers were also successful in ensuring that reorganization was accompanied by adequate building facilities and staffing arrangements. Initially declared opponents of reorganization, the teachers became partners in its implementation because the LEA had given them an alternative to outright and probably fruitless opposition. This cooperation between the LEA and its teachers had, moreover, been for some years an important feature of education in Tynemouth, but its importance was never more clearly demonstrated than over this issue.

Consultation and Influences

In general, at least in more recent times, the principle of consulting teachers has been widely accepted. Lewin (1968) in his study of the twenty Outer London Boroughs found that all had involved teachers and no group had been so widely consulted. Patterns of consultation varied. Some, such as Bromley and Enfield, preferred to consult through teacher organizations while others such as Ealing and Merton put more emphasis on inviting teachers individually to respond. Most went further than simply using existing consultative machinery and created special working parties consisting of teachers and members. In his more detailed study of Merton Lewin found that teachers views were canvassed by the Chief Education Officer even before he produced his report to the schools' sub-committee and well before any other group was involved. Consultation clearly preceded decision taking. Not only were teachers consulted earliest but also most. They were consulted through their professional organizations, but also as individuals, as members of PTAs, as members of such an organization as the Merton branch of CASE and also as coopted members of the Education Committee. As Lewin comments 'Teacher opinion has been the most powerful single pressure on the Education Committee', and all the more so for its remarkable and unusual unanimity 'No governing body or single school staff or head teacher or PTA has felt obliged to ask the Education Committee to reconsider the scheme adopted as a whole or the role one particular school has been asked to play'. This suggests the teachers got the reorganization in the form they wanted but this may have been no more than the form the authority itself wanted and as such tells us nothing about the power of teachers over this issue.

It is, of course, much easier to chronicle the extent of teacher consultation than to assess the impact of such activity. Certainly impact would seem to be minimal where there was very little by way of consultation but the existence of consultation does not necessarily imply corresponding influence. Where strong majority party systems operate opposition from whatever source tends to be ignored. Thus even where as in Rotherham (Fearn 1977) teachers both presented a united front and established improved consultative machinery their influence on a determined council was minor.

In Gateshead (Batley, *et al.* 1970) although there was consultation the influence of teachers' opinion where they were in opposition to those of the Director and the Education Committee seems to have been negligible. In fact, even consultation was limited and the Council interpreted very literally that part of Circular 10/65 which read 'the Secretary of State believes that once the principles and main outlines of a possible plan of reorganization have been formulated there should *follow* a period of close and genuine consultation'. What happened in Gateshead was that there was no real consultation until the Council had made up its mind what it wanted to do and then was quite unprepared to allow subsequent consultations to deter them from their course. They certainly would not have agreed with the views of the Gloucestershire Chief Education Officer that 'The important lesson is that when proposals are first put before governors, teachers or parents they should be suggestions only; that they have not been finally approved by the Authority and are genuinely open to re-examination' (TES 6/10/67).

Parkinson's study of four LEAs supports this view of fairly ineffective teacher influence. He summarizes his findings as 'In every case they took objection to the local Education Authority's plans in detail and in some cases in principle as well. But in no case, either in detail or principle, were the teachers successful. In most cases the Local Education Authority went ahead with its plans despite the reservations of its teachers' (1972, p.36). Again Rigby's (1975) study of reorganization in Crawley concludes that 'There is no evidence that teachers had any significant influence on educational decision making despite the rapidly changing situation in the town which made their intervention possible'. The teachers associations showed no real awareness of the role they might have played. Rigby concludes this failure was partly due to their own docility and narrow horizons and partly LEA policy. The Chief Education Officer did not accept that teachers should play a role in decision making and the Chairman of the Education Committee, a retired brigadier, likened their position to that of sargeants in relation to officers, that is people who would not be consulted about strategy.

Such studies confirm the general impression that although teachers were generally consulted they were not necessarily influential. But exceptions do exist and we have already noted the significance of teachers in Middlesex (Saran, 1973). In Darlington (Batley *et al*, 1970) the movement of teacher opinion in favour in reorganization encouraged a similar change of opinion on the part of the LEA. In

West Ham, Pescheck (1966) found teachers a powerful group and a strong tradition of consultation existed. Three reasons accounts for strong tradition of consultation existed. Three reasons accounted for this situation. Firstly the sympathetic attitude of the Chief Education Officer and his deputy. Secondly, a Labour council and its close association with the trade union movement reflected in an equally sympathetic attitude to union solidarity and rights among council employees. Thirdly, as the result of the unusual policy of almost invariably appointing heads from internal applicants such appointees had a strong self-confidence in their ability to act as legitimate links between an almost exclusively working class community devoid of educational pressure groups and the administration.

White (1974) found a very strong tradition of teacher consultation in Bath. It was their opposition more than anything that led to the abandonment of attempts at reorganization between 1966 and 1968. However in 1969 there was a significant increase in support for comprehensives on the part of the authority. Not least in explaining this was the fact that the new Chairman of the Education Committee was himself a teacher in a comprehensive school in a neighbouring authority. The Chairman's political determination was strengthened by the Director's change of attitude and from now teachers were informed that their role would be advisory only and the council was now determined to proceed with reorganization. Thus while in the earlier period teachers through their opposition had been able to nullify schemes approved by Council sub-committees this was no longer true in the later period. Diminished consultation and influence was related to the growing degree of political decisiveness and authority of the education committee.

Certainly attitudes towards consultation varied widely. In Oxford (Rhodes, 1974) the NUT suffered from its identification by the Conservatives with the Labour Party and exercised little influence. In Brighton (Peterson, 1971) the majority Conservatives were throughout suspicious of unionized approaches to consultation whereas Labour councils as in Hounslow and Leeds favoured such an approach and as a result teachers exercized greater influence in these areas. Authorities had established traditions relating to the extent of teacher consultation and these were major determinants of what was to happen when reorganization became a major issue. In some cases as in Sheffield (Fearn, 1977) reorganization stimulated teachers' demands for improved consultative machinery which were largely met but in many instances established traditions and machinery were more resistant to change. In Manchester (Stern, 1971) concerted and largely united teacher opposition was a major factor causing the abandonment of two plans and the modification of others. Teachers opposed both reorganization in principle and the details of individual schemes. Teachers opposition was used to good effect by the minority Conservative Party which also opposed change. In addition the Chief Education Officer was not fully committed to radical change preferring a more gradualist approach. The teachers also operated jointly with parent groups including sending a joint delegation to the Secretary of State. This combination of forces serving to delay reorganization for several years until 1967. Likewise in Leicester (Mander, 1975) continued teacher opposition was important in preventing reorganization before its amalgamation with Leicestershire.

In Northamptonshire (Eggleston, 1966) teacher opinion being favourable to the plan was the crucial factor in ensuring its acceptance by the education committee. An important background factor being that the traditional pattern of county government was one where sharp divisions on political lines had seldom occurred. This made it necessary for the administration to focus their attention on the views of the teachers' leaders knowing that if they agreed the council would follow suit.

In Birmingham (Isaac-Henry, 1970) teachers played a key part in rejecting Conservative proposals for reorganization because the scheme involved retaining grammar schools. It had been proposed that selection would be on the basis of parental choice guided by teacher advice. Teachers announced they would refuse to operate such a system. In response the council abandoned this but teachers still decided to break off consultations stating they were not prepared to see anything short of a fully comprehensive system. They justified this action by arguing the Conservative plans were political not educational and hence there was no point in further discussions. When the Council sent its proposals to the DES these were rejected and the opposition of the teachers may well have contributed to this result.

There is little evidence of teachers acting as actual initiators of policy. They were legally debarred from being elected as members of their employing authority. However, there was no reason why they should not belong to their local political party and in this capacity there are a few cases of them being influential as policy initiators. Thus Hampton (1970) found in Sheffield that the movement for comprehensive reorganization was in fact led by a group of young Labour teachers who had formed an informal committee with like-minded Council members. Similarly in Reading (Peschek and Brand, 1966) pressure originated in a group of teachers on the General Management Committee of the local Labour Party. In Southampton (White, 1974) prior to Circular 10/65 the only advocates for reorganization within the Labour Group were two young teachers. Similarily in both Doncaster and Sheffield (Fearn, 1977) teachers within the local Labour Party were influential in initiating reorganization. Such small groups of individual teachers often acted as ginger groups persuading other party members of the need for change and drawing attention to what they saw as weaknesses in the system.

Apart from simple pro and anti reorganization positions teachers reacted differently to the various schemes. Any reorganization could threaten the salary, status and working conditions of some teachers and thus many favoured plans which could be introduced with the least disturbance to the status quo. As a result many secondary modern teachers favoured Sixth Form college plans rather than all-through or two tier plans. In this arrangement secondary modern schools would largely maintain their identity continuing to teach the eleven-sixteen age range now including the abler pupils. The all-through system, by contrast, would mean amalgamations of schools and pose problems of tenure for existing heads, deputies and heads of departments. The two tier system would mean that many schools accustomed to teaching 11-16s would now only teach up to age 13. Grammar school teachers generally reacted to Sixth Form schemes favourably if their school was planned to become one and unfavourably if designated otherwise!

Thus the scope for divisions of opinions among teachers was very considerable and had serious repercussions. For example, Peterson (1971) in his study of reorganization in Leeds, Hounslow and Brighton showed that working parties in each case divided on predictable lines. Where a more selective plan was proposed as the compromise, secondary modern teachers withdrew their support. Where a more comprehensive plan was prepared, grammar school teachers refused to agree. Since the working parties failed to agree it is not surprising they had little impact.

Similarly in Bristol (Wood, 1973) there were the usual divisions as a result of which teacher consultative committees found difficulty synthesizing divergent views and producing a coherent viewpoint. This much reduced the impact of such committees. By contrast a good deal of teacher influence in Norwich (Hewitson, 1969) was due to their decision to minimize differences and present a united and unanimous front. This not only showed the degree of teacher feeling on the issue but also encouraged the authority to see some value in consultation. Sheffield teachers (Fearn, 1977) also increased their effectiveness by sinking their differences and working through a joint council which met in advance of the full consultative council in order to prepare agreed statements wherever possible.

Assessing Teacher Influence

It is often argued that teachers, for a number of reasons, would be a powerful group in influencing local authorities. Many officers and members agree that successful reorganization necessitates securing their willing cooperation. Again it has been shown that their occupational concentration in schools makes them relatively easy to organize while their middle-class status makes them good 'joining material'. In addition over this issue their interests both personal and professional are obviously at stake. Also teachers are generally seen as a legitimate interest in educational decision making though LEAs vary in the extent they are prepared to concede this. Furthermore, teachers' presence is institutionalized within the system in various ways. They usually enjoy close relations with the education department and are represented on various committees. Individual teachers may have influence on account of personal relationships with members and officers. Teachers may be important members of local party and pressure groups.

Beer (1965) has argued that the basis of power of successful groups is the dependence of governments on their advice, acquiescence and approval. While it is true that teachers are regarded as knowledgeable and expert, councillors have an alternative source of advice in their education officers and to this extent are not wholly dependent on teachers. As for the second power base, acquiescence, it is doubtful whether teachers in general would actually refuse to operate a scheme which had the approval of the LEA and the DES. Teacher approval, the third power base, was important in the thinking of LEAs many of which went to considerable lengths to make such modifications as the teachers were in favour of. Also the DES took account of teacher opinion in considering whether or not to approve schemes.

The extent of teacher influence varied considerably. Individual authorities had very different attitudes towards the need for consultation and although these were subject to revision they tended to exercize a continuing impact on the degree of teacher power. In most authorities the need to harness the support of teachers was seen as of major importance and to this end teachers became effective partners in the drawing up of schemes.

Much depended on the teachers themselves. In some areas they increased their impact by sinking their differences and presenting a united front to the authority. On occasions this was extended to acting jointly with like-minded parent groups. Where teachers failed to reduce their divisions their opinions were more likely to be discounted. In some instances the teachers' limited conception of their potential role meant that they effectively abdicated any influence they might otherwise have exercized.

Naturally, some teachers were more influential than others. Quite small numbers of teachers, as members of local Labour parties, had on occasions a very considerable influence promoting the comprehensive cause. In other cases it was largely head teachers rather than the rank and file who exercized greatest impact. Certainly, teachers acted as a powerful veto group and their opposition served to persuade some authorities to abandon their proposals for reorganization sometimes for several years. In other instances teacher opposition caused substantial modifications to proposed schemes.

An important factor in all this was the nature of the local party system. Where there was a strong disciplined majority party committed to a definite course of action the impact of teacher opposition was limited to obtaining minor concessions. Thus it is to the influence of political parties we must next turn.

Chapter Five

Party Games:
The Impact of the Political Parties

To understand the behaviour of local parties we need first to know something about the policies and attitudes of their national counterparts. These in turn are closely related to the ideologies existing within those parties. As Bilski (1973, p.197) comments, 'It is my contention that from 1944 the national policies on comprehensive schools adopted by the two parties were largely influenced by the parties' ideologies'.

Traditionally, the Labour Party has always paid lip service to the importance of education and claimed to have a special concern for it in the light of the close relationship between education and the pursuit of equality within society. The party has always espoused a concern for equality of educational opportunity both in the interests of the individual and the wider society. As early as 1918 the party created an Advisory Committee on Education to advise it on long term educational policy. Its early reports showed a clear recognition of the fact that the educational system remained essentially class biased and that the secondary system was primarily based not on the intellectual ability of children but the depth of their parents' pockets. But it was not until 1922 that the party committed itself to the idea of universal free secondary education. The party seemed, nevertheless, to accept that there would be a variety of types of secondary school. During its brief first period of office in 1924 the party went some way towards reform by increasing the number of free places LEAs could offer. This measure was discontinued by the Conservatives and illustrated the difference of attitude between the two parties, the Conservatives retaining their elitist view of education and a preoccupation with preserving grammar school standards for the few. Attempts by the second Labour government in 1929 to increase opportunities for secondary education were sabotaged by the grave financial crisis and the activities of a Conservative dominated House of Lords in rejecting its Education Bill. The main achievement being again raising the percentage of free places from 40 per cent to 50 per cent. The ensuing Conservative administration, however, replaced the system of free places with one of special places which in effect meant that working class children had to be 'exceptionally clever and exceptionally poor' to benefit from secondary education.

Early Consensus

Although educationalists in the twenties and thirties had supported the idea of a common secondary school the official philosophy of the period as exemplified by the Hadow (1926) and Spens (1938) Reports all implied a variety of secondary schools. As pointed out above the philosophy also prevailed within the Labour Party. And if in 1939 the party's Advisory Committee on Education supported the idea of the multi-lateral school and went so far as to recommend it to the London Labour Party neither the Committee nor the party as a whole were strongly in support of the idea.

The Hadow Report was important insofar as it advocated eleven as the dividing line between primary and secondary education and argued that selection for different types of secondary school should be made on the basis of examination.

> While we think that all children should enter some type of post primary school at the age of 11+, it will be necessary to discover in each case the type most suitable to a child's abilities and interests. For this purpose a written examination should be held and also, wherever possible, an oral examination. A written psychological test might also be specially employed in dealing with borderline cases, or where a discrepancy has been observed between the results of the written examination and the teacher's estimate of proficiency (Ibid, p.178).

The report had concluded in favour of a bipartite system of secondary modern and grammar schools but growing support for secondary technical schools encouraged the subsequent Spens Report to propose a tripartite system. Despite favourable evidence from both the National Association of Labour Teachers and the TUC the Report had little favourable to say for multilateral schools. It assembled no less than six arguments against them mostly relating to their assumed size and the dangers of one side, such as the academic, developing at the expense of another. Its conclusion being:

> . . . the general adoption of the multilateral idea would be too subversive a change to be made in a long established system, especially in view of the extent to which this system has been expanded in recent years by the building of new Grammar schools and Technical schools (Ibid, p.291).

The tripartite system was accepted in the 1943 White Paper on Educational Reconstruction and further endorsed by the Norwood Report published a few days later. This Report served to make tripartism a doctrine with an assumed psychological legitimacy arguing as it did for the existence of three separate types of mind and the necessity for corresponding types of school. The 1944 Education Act avoided reference to tripartism and left open the question of the organization of secondary schooling. R. A. Butler, the main architect of the Act, has been reported (Boyle, 1972) describing how his chief parliamentary draftsman, Sir Granville Ram, assured him that the Act could meet the needs of at least a generation provided it did not seek to exclude experiments with multilateral schools. Alice Bacon explained the omission to the protest from the National Executive of the Labour Party at the reference to tripartism in the 1943 White Paper.

Despite the 1944 Act's reticence on the issue Circular 73 (1945) assumed LEAs development plans would be on tripartite lines and proceeded to propose percentages for each type of school. Thus it assumed between seventy and seventy-five per cent of children would go to modern schools with the remainder going to grammar and technical schools. The same tripartite scheme was expounded in another Ministry publication, 'The Nations' Schools — their Plan and Purpose' (1945). This document was repudiated by delegates at the 1946 Labour Party Annual Conference but its replacement the following year,'The New Secondary Education', also emphasized the tripartite system. Various attempts from within the Labour Party to bring about a change of mind from their leaders brought little response. Ellen Wilkinson, Labour's first post war Minister of Education, remained unimpressed by the arguments and placed her faith in the achievement of parity of resources between different kinds of secondary school leading, it was hoped, to parity of esteem.

The Ministry was determined, despite party pressures, to defend the grammar school and avoid anything other than cautious experimentation with comprehensive schools. There was a distinct lack of direct encouragement for comprehensive schools and an implicit bias towards the continuation of tripartism. The Ministry realized that grammar schools could not share the same catchment areas as comprehensive schools and this further hardened opposition to the latter. Wilkinson's successor, George Tomlinson, was also averse to schemes involving 'tampering' with grammar schools. Neither Wilkinson nor Tomlinson had particularly original minds or any great capacity for innovation but it is also fair to point out that during their period of office there were many other major tasks needing urgent attention apart from this one. Many Labour politicians were themselves products of the grammar school tradition and had a nostalgic commitment to it. They believed that it did make a real contribution to providing equality of opportunity for working class children. Politicians of all parties found difficulty in believing other than that as all children were not of equal ability and aptitude they were best educated in different types of school. This, after all, was the general view of educationalists themselves. As for equality of opportunity it seemed a truism that this was achieved by a system of 'objective' testing whereby every child had an equal chance of obtaining a grammar school place. Further, those 'allocated' other than to grammar schools would have the opportunity of being educated in secondary modern or technical schools specially designed to meet their needs and it was assumed ensuring parity of esteem with the grammar schools. What such thinking ignored was that such schools were fundamentally designed for working class children going into jobs requiring little by way of educational achievement and thus could never achieve parity of esteem with the more prestigious selective schools. The persistent refusal of Labour Ministers of Education to fall into line with party demands are best explained in terms of traditional concern for the future of grammar schools; the official philosophy of tripartism and its supposed psychological and moral justification; a limited conception of equality of opportunity and an awareness of the administrative task involved in reorganizing an educational system at a time of great change anyway.

This support for selective education was also reflected in the vast majority of LEAs. A survey of development plans (Thompson, 1952) in three-quarters of LEAs revealed that very few secondary school places would be in comprehensive schools. Those LEAs deviating from the tripartite pattern fell into one of two categories. Firstly there were large urban authorities such as London, Coventry and Reading which were motivated by political reasons. Of the five urban authorities with the largest percentage of school population planned for comprehensive school four were Labour controlled. Secondly, there were rural authorities often with scattered populations which wanted to create comprehensive schools to meet their particular educational problems. Of the five rural authorities with the largest percentage of school population planned for comprehensive school four were Conservative controlled. However, the number of comprehensive and multilateral schools built remained very small and they were regarded very much as experimental and the exception to the norm.

Labour Party Initiatives

At the same time there was developing within the Labour Party growing unease about the selective principle. There was, among certain members at least, a growing awareness of the inconsistency between tripartism and the party's commitment to equality of educational opportunity. The illusion of parity of esteem between schools whose products entered such completely different career patterns was becoming increasingly apparent. And so was the realization that the selective system was perpetuating the divisions and disparities that had separated elementary and secondary education in the pre-war period. Each of the three types of post-war school represented a continuation of earlier traditions which inevitably influenced public attitudes towards them. The grammar school represented a continuation of the secondary school which had enjoyed the prestige of superior premises and staffing and the educational and occupational destinations of their pupils. By contrast, the secondary modern schools represented a continuation of the senior schools developed from the upper forms of elementary schools while the technical schools had developed from the junior technical schools. Critics of the selective system characterized it as epitomizing inequality of opportunity, of provision and ultimately of concern. The 1950 Labour Party Conference called upon the government to commit itself to the comprehensive principle and final authorization was given the following year in 'A Policy for Secondary Education'.

Thus Labour went into opposition with a reaffirmed commitment to ending selective secondary education. But the party was now in opposition and after six years in office there were little more than a dozen comprehensive schools in existence. Lack of enthusiasm among Labour leaders both nationally and locally, distrust on the part of Ministry and LEA officials, and doubts held by the teaching profession had prevented all but the most minor changes.

In opposition, discussion of the issue centred on whether a Labour government should proceed with reorganization on a compulsory basis or not. The National Association of Labour Teachers took the view that compulsion was necessary and a similar line was taken by Alice Bacon arguing that the public were sufficiently sympathetic to accept such a line. The example of Conservative Ministers blocking the introduction of comprehensive schools by LEAs served further to increase support for this hard line. Others in the party, sensed neither the public nor LEAs were yet sufficiently in favour of reorganization and that an educational campaign was the first priority. This seemed born out by a 1957 opinion poll carried out for the Labour Party which revealed that only ten per cent of those questioned felt that socially segregated education was undesirable and the majority of parents were basically satisfied with the existing educational system. The party, in these circumstances, had to weigh very carefully whether it could afford to use compulsion against LEAs many of which both strongly and sincerely would oppose reorganization. In particular, there was uncertainty about the exact future of the grammar school for which a great deal of public support, both inside and outside the party, was apparent. While some within the party envisaged coexistence, others saw their disappearance as essential.

During the early 1960s the party began an attempt to win over public support for the non-selective system. Dropping the traditional ideological and class approach as electorally unprofitable they focussed more on the drawbacks of the selective system in terms of the national wastage of talent. An opinion poll in 1962 encouraged party leaders by showing general public support for their policies. When the party regained office two years later the gap between ideology and policy of the 1945-51 period was not allowed to recur.

Rubinstein and Simon (1973, p.119) have argued that 'The movement towards comprehensive education is bigger than particular political parties and has taken shape historically without the support of any of the major parties. Fundamentally this movement is a reflection of deep seated economic and social changes'. But if in retrospect the Labour Party has not been the only force pressing for the end of the selective system it has been a particularly important pressure in politicizing demands for reform. There was a consistent championing of the ideal of equality of educational opportunity though over time this ideal had to be redefined as what earlier seemed to be equality proved illusory. Indeed this process has by no means yet run its full course. But if as Parkinson (1970, p.127) concludes the party 'has persistently exercized pressure for reforms intended to make English secondary education less elitist and class oriented' it remains true that this pressure had not in the main been exercised through Parliamentary channels. As Kogan (1975) notes Parliament has hardly been involved in the whole process. In the period 1964-71 only seven parliamentary questions were asked concerning the abolition of the 11+. Also the position during the period of the previous Labour government, 1945-51, seems according to Fenwicke (1976, p.58) to have been little different. 'The most significant aspect of parliamentary pressure for comprehensive schools at this period is its relative insignificance; no more than half a dozen Labour MPs came out in support of comprehensive schools throughout the first Labour government.' Far greater pressure was exerted on the Labour leaders by the party's Annual Conference, by such Labour MPs as Alice Bacon and Margaret Herbison and the National Association of Labour Teachers which kept the issue alive within the party and eventually brought about its acceptance by the leadership.

Conservative Responses

It would be wrong, as is often done, to describe the Conservative Party's attitude to education as wholly pragmatic and non-ideological. Conservatives have adopted implicit ideological stances over such issues as parental freedom, traditional standards and their own interpretation of equality of opportunity. Furthermore, it would be misleading to assume neither party had any concern for the values of their opponents and the degrees of agreement and division between the parties varied considerably over time.

During the 1940s the Conservative Party nationally did not favour comprehensive schools and by the 1951 election their attitude had become increasingly critical and spokesmen such as R. A. Butler and Quintin Hogg emphasized the Hadow line in calling for a variety of secondary schools. The Conservative Minister of Education, Florence Horsburgh, while having strong reservations about 'large, soulless educational factories' was willing to allow limited experiments, such as in Coventry. Where schemes involved the absorption of grammar schools the attitude was much harder. Her successor, David Eccles, took an early opportunity to reassure the grammar schools. 'One must choose between justice and equality, for it is impossible to apply both principles at once. Those who support comprehensive schools prefer equality. Her Majesty's Government prefer justice. My colleagues and I will never agree to the assassination of the grammar schools'. In 1958 the government's White Paper 'Secondary Education for All, "A New Drive" ', stated that experiments with comprehensive schools could only be permitted in country districts with sparse populations and in new housing estates with no existing schools. As Benn and Simon (1972, p.52) have written 'There was no official encouragement for the development of comprehensive schools after 1951 by the Conservative government which then took office and was to remain in office until 1964'. Apart from its commitment to preserving the grammar school tradition the Conservatives made frequent references to preserving what they interpreted as parental freedom of choice. There were also references to the need to preserve LEA freedom of choice. It portrayed Labour's proposed policies as attempting to impose a uniform central pattern on LEAs, very few of which would, of their own free will, have adopted such a pattern. To the extent Labour's own defence of the comprehensive school was in social as well as educational terms it was possible for the Conservatives to attack their approach as ideological, while seeming to deny the equally ideological nature of their own thinking.

Nevertheless, during the 1950s politicians of both parties were becoming increasingly aware of the disadvantages of the selective system. With the introduction of the General Certificate of Education, designed specifically for grammar schools, secondary modern schools began to enter their ablest pupils and the results undermined the theory that such children, having failed the 11+, lacked the innate capacity to benefit from an academic education. A related development was the growing pressure from parents of all classes of children for them to be able to gain qualifications which were now being seen as increasingly necessary for vocational purposes. The Crowther Report (1959) drew attention to the growth of the proportion of highly skilled jobs and the corresponding decline in the proportion of unskilled vacancies in the economy. Also, in the 1950s, an increasing volume of sociological evidence pointed to the relationship between social class and educational opportunity and cast doubts on the 'objective' nature of the selection tests. At the same time psychologists were beginning to concede that the constancy of IQ on which selection at eleven had been justified, was less than had previously been believed. In addition evidence showed that LEAs varied considerably in the number of grammar school places they provided.

Thus variations in pass rate at 11+ depended on arbitrary differences in the numbers of grammar school places provided by individual LEAs, which ranged from eight per cent to over forty per cent provision. In addition there was evidence that as many as ten per cent of children were being wrongly allocated and yet provision for late transfer operated in relatively few cases (Yates and Newnes, 1957). Equality of educational opportunity was increasingly seen to be an empty slogan. And if this was so, not only was there individual unfairness but also wastage of national talent as the Crowther Report (1959) so amply demonstrated. Additionally, with the actual establishment of comprehensive schools discussion about them shifted from the realm of speculation to that of practical experience. A considerable number of such schools were seen as successful, both in terms of their examination results and also their ability to retain children after the school leaving age. National politicians could hardly ignore the growing numbers of large LEAs such as Manchester, Liverpool, Lancashire and Yorkshire which were thinking in terms of comprehensive reorganization. By 1961 London had fifty-nine comprehensive schools taking fifty-three per cent of the secondary population. Of these, twenty-two had been purpose built. The first of these to open, Kidbrooke, attracted a great deal of interest in other LEAs and was influential in persuading some of them to take a more favourable view of comprehensive education. Leicestershire was also influential in showing the possibility of reorganization without massive rebuilding, and without antagonizing the Ministry or local parents and teachers.

The selective system assumed that the level of measured ability remained constant from the age of secondary transfer, that only a small proportion of children could benefit from an 'academic' education and that separation into different types of school on the basis of ability was educationally efficient. All three assumptions came under increasing challenge as did traditional definitions of equality of opportunity. Growing numbers of parents, including many middle class parents, became increasingly concerned at what they saw as the unfairness and arbitrariness of the system.

The Conservative Party's reactions to criticism of the selective system was largely limited to attempts to raise the status of the secondary modern schools as by encouraging the creation of GCE streams within them. The 1964 Education Act further permitted LEAs to introduce greater flexibility into the system by creating middle schools. But if in the late 1960s Conservative politicians were coming to recognize faults in the selective system they retained a concern not to jeopardize what they saw as its achievements. Thus speaking in 1967 the leader of the party stated 'Perhaps in the past there has been a tendency on the part of governments and teachers to concentrate too much on the ablest children and not enough on the average. This tendency is now being corrected and rightly so. But we must be sure that in concentrating on those who have not had a chance in the past we do not neglect those who could and should be excelling'. Conservatives were coming to realize that the 11+ was increasingly unpopular both among educationalists and parents. It was becoming as Benn and Simon (1972) christened it 'the Achilles heel of the tripartite system'. At the 1966 Party Conference the party's education spokesman Edward Boyle, stated that 'the Conservative

Party has accepted the weight of evidence against selection as early as eleven or twelve'. Writing six years later Boyle (1972, p.34) wrote 'Conservative policy at the time of the 1964 election went a long way short of saying that all Local Education Authorities should reorganize . . . but it recognized that many, probably most, local authorities would reorganize. The pressure for change was strong and had come to stay'. Nevertheless, there was a great deal of resentment over the policy contained in Circular 10/65 and when the Labour government proposed legislation in 1970 the Times Educational Supplement, reporting the ensuing Parliamentary debate commented, 'There are few issues on which the two sides of the Commons are so deeply divided'. This hardening of attitudes was further illustrated by the way in which the Conservatives withdrew in 1970 Circulars 10/65 and 10/66. There was no prior consultation and the new Secretary of State Margaret Thatcher explained tersely 'consultation is only meaningful where you intend to be influenced by the representations'. On several occasions Boyle had suggested that the next Conservative government would not necessarily withdraw Circular 10/65. This growing consensus between the two parties was quickly ruptured by Thatcher whose hard line polarized the situation once more and produced a renewed emphasis on the preservation of parental choice and standards of academic excellence.

Whatever the attitudes of the national parties it would be wrong to assume too close a relationship between these and those of their local counterparts. Even on so party political an issue as this differences of opinion prevailed and therefore it is necessary to move from the national perspective to consider the roles and attitudes of the local parties.

Parties and Local Government

While the literature of political science is replete with studies of political parties these tend to focus on the organization and types of party system. The dynamics of the policy making process within parties has received scant attention and even less has been devoted to policy making within local parties. Bulpitt's (1967) work was very much a pioneering study and even now, over ten years later, the literature on local parties is surprisingly limited. This is unfortunate as

Bulpitt's work as carried out in the period 1955-60, was limited to boroughs, all of which were in one part of the country, north-west England. Today, we have no equivalent study of parties within the reorganized system of local government. Indeed since Bulpitt we have no major study which focusses exclusively on parties and the only references are within more general case studies such as those referred to in this work. The comment by the Maud Report (1967) that 'the place of party politics is much debated but very little documented' remains largely true.

Opinions differ sharply on the advantages and disadvantages of party politics in local government but it is a quite pointless exercise to assemble and weigh these as if the exercize will have the slightest effect on the reality that most and a growing number of authorities operate on party lines. Yet the exact influence of parties on local policy making is difficult to assess. Bulpitt's study, for example, suggests that local parties were more concerned with the possession of power than its actual exercize. That there was more interest in obtaining positions than in using these to pursue particular policies. Similarly, Donnison's (1976) case studies give little support for the idea of local parties as major initiators of policy. The Maud Committee's (1967) surveys found that most councillors were of the opinion that party politics played a much smaller part in local government than was generally believed. Heclo (1969, p.194) in his study of Manchester councillors quoted as typical the comment of one Labour Councillor that 'Eighty per cent of council work is administrative not political. On my Committee, for example, I find I'm voting as often with the Tories as with the members of my own party'. By contrast Boaden (1971) concludes that the main variations in the provision of services do arise from party politics. How local authorities respond to needs and how services are provided depend largely on the influence of party on councillors' dispositions. Labour councils, for example, were found to be bigger spenders on the bigger services and had a general tendency to favour higher standards. His evidence also suggested that party affects priorities both between services and within them. In the area of education Boaden found a close relationship between Labour control and above average spending and progress on secondary reorganization. Hampton (1970, p.65) also found that 'The political party groups are undoubtedly the most important influence on the attitudes of members of the Sheffield

City Council'.

Councillors' involvement with a party makes it more likely that the party's ideology will affect their receptiveness and responsiveness to different demands. Studies such as Dearlove's (1973) suggest that councillors' party political viewpoints lead them to expose themselves to sources of information that will serve to reinforce their existing beliefs. They also suggest that their main source of information is the council itself and particularly members of their own party. Parties also influence the selection of candidates, accepting some and rejecting others. The Maud Committee found that about one third of existing councillors came into local government through connections with political parties and two thirds were members of such parties. Younger councillors, in particular, were even more likely to have come into local government through association with a party. Over sixty per cent of borough councillors were asked to stand by a party and believed parties did not often look outside their own ranks when searching for new recruits. We know very little about the criteria used for such selection and the whole area of party influence on the recruitment, and, equally important, the socialization of councillors is one where much basic research remains to be done.

The relationships between councillors and their parties varies considerably. Members, for example, vary in the extent to which they are active within the party. Parties vary in the extent to which they determine member behaviour. The relations between the party group on the council and the local party organization also varies considerably. Also party systems vary by locality. Some areas are highly competitive such as Jones (1969) found in Wolverhampton while others such as West Ham (Peschek and Brand, 1966) have equally long traditions of one party rule. Thus in discussing the impact of local parties on decision making it is crucial to remember the diversity of party systems within local government (Jones, 1975). Bulpitt (1967) distinguishes between negative and positive party systems. In the former case party labels are used no more than as electoral devices and not as a means of controlling councillor behaviour or the distribution of positions. In a positive party system party meetings determine policy and voting behaviour and patronage positions are distributed on party lines. Clearly there is a continuum from those authorities where elections are not even contested on party lines through to those where they are but once elected members drop their party labels and act as independents through to where party allegiance determines decision making in nearly all areas of council activity.

The structural reforms of nineteenth century local government produced largely socially homogenous areas which typically returned one party or group to power for long periods. But the reorganization of 1974 destroyed many of the largely rural authorities and all the county boroughs in the attempt to end the administrative division between town and country. By doing this it has ushered in very new styles of party politics in which the urban rather than the traditional rural style seems more likely to prevail. This system is characterized as tending towards a competitive, disciplined and more policy oriented party system. One study (Jennings, 1975) of the effects of reorganization in three counties on educational policy making discerned a reduction in the numbers of independent councillors, increased party solidarity, greater political control of cooption, increased use of whipping and a hardening of party lines and the increased use of the policy and resources committee as a vital party control mechanism.

The increasingly typical pattern for local parties is one in which candidates are selected by local ward parties, where members meet regularly both as a group and at committee level to decide policy in advance and leading members form a policy committee to give leadership and coordination. This is a pattern which has been common for many years in our larger urban areas and can, in part, be linked to the role of the Labour Party in local government. Although it would be misleading to attribute the development of parties in local government to the involvement of the Labour Party in local affairs such involvement was not without its effects. Jones (1969, p.67) notes that in Wolverhampton Labour control of the council in 1945 led to the party acting with regard to the council as the Labour Party did nationally towards Parliament. Although this led to initial protests from the Conservative Party, 'Yet by the late 1950's, realizing they could not defeat Labour or indeed run the Council along traditional lines of sharing offices and responsibility, the Conservatives had adopted these very techniques and even perfected them more effectively than the Labour Party. Regular group meetings were held at the same time as Labour's; shadow chairmen watched their opposite numbers in the Labour Party and a policy committee was established to act as a kind of Shadow Cabinet'. Outside the Council the effects were to increase the numbers of contested seats, the numbers of people voting and to almost eliminate the chances of independents being elected. Jones found that Labour Councillors felt they owed their seat to the party and as a result saw it as essential, beneficial and an important object of their loyalty. By contrast, Conservative councillors were less likely to come onto the council through party activity and thus devoted less time and support to the party seeing themselves as ward representatives more than party representatives. The Labour Party's commitment to disciplined, bloc voting was the outcome of having a municipal policy which required concerted action to implement. They voted together not because they were coerced but on account of common agreement over policy. Discussion within the group was free but once a decision was reached members generally accepted their duty to support it. If this was the tradition within the Labour Party it certainly was not the Conservative tradition. Traditionally the Conservatives did not profess distinctive municipal programmes or act as a disciplined group. But the need to be more effective in the face of the Labour Party caused the Conservatives to abandon their traditions in favour of those of that party.

Similarly, Hampton (1970, p.61) in his study of Sheffield writes that since 1919:

> the Council has been managed on strict party lines with regular party group meetings before the full Council meeting to enable party policies to be decided. Both parties expect their members to support the decision of the group within the council chamber and whips are appointed to supervize the group management and discipline. The party which obtains the majority on the City Council controls all the policy making for the city and appoints its members to the chairmanship and deputy chairmanship of all Committees.

In situations such as this the centre of power is no longer the council chamber but the private meetings of the party group. Thus Marmion (1967) comments in his study of Liverpool, 'The efficient parts of the Local Education Authority are to be found in the caucuses of the major parties'. It may even be that the real power lies with an inner group of the most senior party members and indeed some of the case studies point to the existence of single dominant individuals.

The party group will usually arrange its meetings to precede official meetings both at committee and council level. The group would be involved both in discussing future committee decisions and screening decisions already made in committee and deciding whether to support or oppose them in council. Thus party groups ensure their views are made clear at all levels of decision making. As Wiseman (1967, p.72) comments 'The Council Group, consisting of all the majority party councillors and aldermen, in the supreme controlling body in towns where local government is run on party lines'. If we are right in arguing that more local authorities are being run on party lines and that the style of local parties is increasingly disciplined and programmatic parties must play an increasingly important role in policy making. Thus Jennings (1976) argues that educational policy making takes places in an increasingly closed and party dominated system. The majority parties firmly control the committee system as well as the full council. Officers are required to tailor their proposals to the attitudes and priorities of the ruling party. Education chairmen are expected to operate within the guidelines laid down by party leaders. Coopted members and governors are selected on largely party lines. The degree and effectiveness of consultation with outside groups is as determined by the majority party.

Local Parties and Secondary Reorganization

Certainly on an issue such as secondary reorganization which so captured the attention of both major parties one would expect to see parties exercizing a major influence over policy making. And yet the relationship was far from straight forward. The absence of a simple relationship between party affiliation and attitude towards reorganization is clearly illustrated in the case of Leeds (Fenwicke and Woodthorpe, 1980). Throughout much of the fifties and early sixties the majority Labour group was reluctant to reorganize stressing as late as 1962 the impossibility of ending selection. Pressure from the local Labour Party plus the election nationally of a Labour government eventually forced the group into action. However, before the plans were approved by the DES the Tories seized power. In the event the new Tory education chairman proved equally if not more commited to reorganization than his predecessor. In both

Manchester (Stern, 1971) and Sheffield (Fearn, 1977) local Labour parties although exercizing control for long periods were too internally divided to make much progress until well into the sixties. Hampton (1970) in Sheffield found the leading members of the Labour Party, including the Chairman of the Education Committee, were far from convinced that selection should go. Here, as elsewhere, opposition came mainly from older members and one explanation of this is that it was often these people who in earlier days had established the existing selective system. In Sheffield, as in several other cases, the movement in favour of reorganization was led by the younger members of the Labour Party.

The example of the London County Council, of course, shows an example of a strong political will combined with a tightly controlled dominant party forging ahead with reorganization. But generally only a few Labour authorities such as London and Middlesex made such early attempts to reorganize. Birmingham, for example, was continuously Labour controlled from 1952 to 1966 but made no attempt to alter the system until prodded by Circular 10/65. Reactions to this Circular by the outer London Boroughs tended to follow party lines. Conservative strongholds such as Kingston, Harrow, Sutton and Richmond firmly resisted and of the other Boroughs which had not submitted proposals by 1967 seven were Conservative controlled. Labour councils such as Enfield, Bexley and Brent pushed ahead. But here also there were exceptions to the pattern. Merton, although Conservative controlled, pushed ahead with reorganization and Lewin (1968) comments 'It is hard to see more than one motive in action in the decision to reorganize on comprehensive lines — that of the educational merits of comprehensive schools'. Both the sub-committee, the Education Committee and the full Council had all voted unanimously in favour and there was clear inner and inter party agreement. Conservative councils such as Leicestershire, Shropshire, Staffordshire and Oxfordshire all decided on reorganization on educational grounds and in the light of their particular local circumstances. Thus Rigby's (1975) study of Crawley illustrates how a Conservative council could be persuaded by a Labour councillor to experiment with comprehensive schools. This councillor, 'was careful to appear non-doctrinaire ... and he stressed that he was not suggesting a comprehensive system for the whole county, merely a limited experiment in an area which offered favourable opportunities'. He persuaded the Education Committee to visit Middlesex where they saw comprehensives operating under very favourable conditions and not competing with existing grammar schools. Further encouraged by their own Chief Education Officer, the authority allowed the building of its first comprehensive school in 1957 and gradually extended the system throughout its area.

Writing in the context of the early 1960s Pedley (1963) commented that outside London the provision of comprehensive schools fell into two quite distinct categories. First, within rural areas where its evolution owed little or nothing to party politics and a great deal to the logic of the situation. Secondly, in urban areas where party political pressures were the dominant factor even, in the opinion of some, despite the logic of the local situation.

Also local disputes were not always simple party confrontations. Conservative parents were often worried about their own children's chances of grammar school selection while some Labour parents were strong defenders of the grammar school system. In Sheffield (Hampton, 1970) both the Conservatives and Labour parties were very divided on the issue and conflict within the parties was as important as that between them. Nor did the loss of many Labour controlled councils in the late 1960s generally result in the abandonment of comprehensive plans. Only in a few cases was all progress halted and more commonly it was more a matter of things slowing down. The Conservative party, locally at least, was more divided on this issue than is commonly supposed. Many Conservative LEAs fell fairly readily into line with the policy of reorganization. Boyle was known to be not unsympathetic and teacher and public opinion were both coming increasingly to this viewpoint. In Sheffield (Hampton, ibid.) for example, the changeover from Labour to Conservative control in the middle of planning for reorganization did not effect the final decision to proceed. Apart from the reasons mentioned above they did not want to perpetuate indecision about the city's educational future by entering a battle with the DES. The local Conservative party was in a very difficult position, their strongest supporters were in favour of the selective system while the party felt such a policy would loose it the key marginal seats in the impending local elections. Regan (Rhodes, 1972) commenting on the issue within the outer London Boroughs feels that delays in implementing schemes were mainly due to financial stringency and physical problems though admitting Conservative lack of enthusiasm could capitalize on such factors. In Southampton (White, 1974) Labour lost control at a crucial point just following DES approval of their scheme. The local Conservative party was committed in its own election manifesto to preserving the grammar schools. Yet due to a mixture of apathy and divisions within its own ranks and the opinion of local teachers Labour's scheme was not substantially modified in any way. The fact that the party had been out of office for many years meant that the new Chairman and Vice-Chairman of the Education Committee were relatively inexperienced and this must have militated against overthrowing Labour's carefully worked out plans — especially as these were strongly supported by the Chief Education Officer. The Chairman and Vice-Chairman visited London to meet two Conservative MPs who had a deep interest in educational issues, Charles Morrison and Richard Hornby. They advised that any attempt to reverse the scheme and reintroduce selection would not secure the backing of the party leadership. Edward Boyle also commented that he thought the scheme a good one. This combination of circumstances resulted in the scheme being proceeded with despite the local Conservatives election commitment to preserve selection.

This case shows how the ideological stance of local parties often had to be modified in the light of local conditions and the opinions of Chief Education Officers, DES, parents and teachers. The extent to which this was true depending on the nature of the local party system. When the ruling party was disciplined and determined the role of officers, opposition parties and other groups was correspondingly reduced In Gateshead (Batley *et al.,* 1970) for example, the Labour party was long entrenched and very oligarchic. The opposition party made no real contribution to policy decisions and parent and teacher groups played little part either. The reorganization was largely the work of two leading Labour councillors. In Southampton (White, 1974) the Council was largely controlled by a disciplined Labour party and once policy decisions were taken, speeches and voting followed the party line. This combined with a largely passive local community enabled the party's leaders to exercize an elitist authority with little criticism from their own party or others. Consultation was minimal with teachers and parents and the role of the Chief Education Officer was very much that of advising on points of detail.

The Labour majority had the power, took a clear policy decision and wanted a speedy settlement anticipating, rightly, a defeat in the forthcoming local elections. By contrast, White found in Bath a situation where not only was there no single majority party but very little tradition of disciplined party support. Schemes approved by sub-committee were frequently rejected in council and some members were unwilling to support in council proposals already approved in sub-committee by their own party education leaders. Each party had its own attitude towards reorganization and several years had to pass before the opposed attitudes aligned sufficiently to make agreement between the parties possible. In these circumstances parties were weak and power dispersed. Thus in Southampton majority control, a political will for change and a dominant education leader, ensured speedy approval of the authority's plans while in Bath a multiparty system in which it proved difficult to obtain either political consensus or discipline made effective policy making also difficult.

Much of the evidence seems to suggest that a great deal of the time and energy of party groups is spent in vetting recommendations originating in committees. But it is important to note that this could remain essentially a negative control and is quite distinct from the power to initiate policy. It must not, therefore, be assumed that party groups are generally initiators of policy and their role may be the more modest one of deciding whether to accept or reject others' initiatives. Such initiatives could equally stem from officers, committee chairmen or more likely a combination of both. Evidence submitted to the Maud Committee (1967) from a large number of Clerks stressed that although political ideas are filtered through party groups they usually originate in individual service committees. Thus it does not follow that the existence of disciplined parties effectively locates power within the party. Even in a situation of tight and effective party control there are two possibilities. On the one hand, it could mean that the party has set up the necessary mechanisms for implementing its *own* policies. On the other hand, it could mean that while the party creates the mechanisms they are no more than an effective means of transforming others' initiatives into effective policies. In short, political parties can be conceived of as goal achieving mechanisms for a number of different groups from any of which initiatives may spring. This is more realistic than the traditional Burkean notion of parties as groups of people banded together to promote the public welfare upon some principle on which they were all agreed. Local authority policy decisions are influenced by a very wide variety of factors. It cannot be assumed that merely because these are organized through party mechanisms that the resulting decisions are a product of coherent and consistent party beliefs. If parties are conceived of more as goal achieving mechanisms we need to ask whose goals are they being used to achieve and this leads us into a discussion of the roles of members and officers as policy initiators.

Chapter Six

Roles and Relationships: the Case of Councillors and Officers

Most of the standard works on local government pay little attention to the role of councillors. Fortunately, reports such as Maud (1967) and Bains (1972) have attached considerable importance to the question of councillor's roles and a number of other studies have now extended this interest.

The traditional description of the member's role is in terms of an elected representative but this is a more complex role than might at first sight appear. The Maud Committee found that councillors were only too well aware of the facts of public indifference and ignorance regarding local government matters. Asked how they found out about public attitudes and needs by far the largest channel of communication was informal contacts. Election campaigns played a very small part and although political parties played a major role in the selection and promotion of councillors they were seen as playing a minor role in providing information on public attitudes. Some councillors acknowledged having very few contacts with the public. Ten per cent said they had seen no electors in the last month and nearer a third fewer than four such contacts in the period. Furthermore, it by no means follows that information so derived will provide the sole or even the main motivation for councillors' decisions and the sense of public need obtained in this way will provide part only of their reasons for deciding how to act to help shape council policy. Feelings that electors are poorly informed and often apathetic may well undermine the importance councillors attach to such expressed needs and opinions. Eighty per cent of councillors felt that the public did not know enough to get a balanced picture of the way the council conducts its affairs.

Newton's (1976) study of Birmingham councillors found that almost half saw themselves as relatively free and independent agents elected to exercize their own conscience and judgement and act according to *their* assessment of situations. They justified this not so much in terms of the silence of public opinion as its diversity and the need to make one's own mind up in the face of conflicting opinions. This conception of role was most common among the more experienced and senior members. Newer councillors were more likely to see themselves giving greater weight to public opinion and in the position more of a delegate. Councillors' attitude to pressure groups are linked to their view of their representative role. Councillors who see themselves in the delegate role are most likely to accept the value and legitimacy of pressure groups in presenting organized opinion on local issues. Those who see themselves as independent agents are more likely to devalue this contribution seeing them as narrow, self-opinionated, and unrepresentative.

Councillors generally are not political entrepreneurs. They do not usually have to engage in a continuous dialogue with their market, the public, to see what will sell and have little need to invest any significant amount of resources in trying to discern or mould public opinion. They have limited need to promote policies reflecting the interests of their constituents in order to maintain politicial office. Of councillors interviewed in Chelsea and Kensington (Dearlove, 1973) seventy-six per cent did not think that the policies of their local party were important in determining election outcomes. Another study (Peterson and Kantor, 1977, p.211) found that only eleven per cent of councillors in Brighton, Hounslow and Leeds felt that local issues affected the outcome of local elections and concluded: 'It is hard to escape the conclusion that local politicians pay little attention to organized groups, democratic rituals and the local press because voters pay little specific attention to local politicians'.

The Power of the few

As well as his role conception of his relationship to the public, the member also has a conception of his role in regard to the work of the council. In Newton's study (ibid) only a quarter expressed a preference for involvement in broad policy making as against individual grievances and problems. The preference for broad policy was commonest among more senior members and Labour rather than Conservative councillors. The implication of such a large percentage of members seeing themselves as unpaid social workers being that a relatively small circle of members largely control major policy decisions.

Newton distinguishes between five role types. The parochials whose interests centre on individual problems within their own ward and are the least ideological and partisan section of the council. They are, however, most likely to follow the lead of the more senior members of their party on policy issues. Secondly, are those who see themselves as ombudsmen for the entire locality. Thirdly, and least significant numerically, are those who see their function as acting as spokesmen for people in their ward over policy issues, acting largely as delegates. Most interesting from our point of view are the two remaining groups, policy advocates and policy brokers. Both are mainly concerned with major policy issues but differ in terms of their conception of their roles as representatives. Policy advocates are ideologues with a greater commitment to politics than any other group. Policy brokers are most likely to see themselves as performing the classical political brokerage roles of mediating between different interests and producing compromises. These last two groups constitute the most influential body on the council and are almost twice as likely to be Labour as Conservative. Newton explains this in terms of different party conceptions of the nature of the political and social world. Conservative group members tended to assume that each individual is largely master of his own fate and thus the member's main job is to help with 'deserving' individual cases. By contrast Labour group members would regard themselves as more sensitive to the effect of socio-economic structures on individual's lives and thus the member's main job is to be concerned with public policy making. Heclo's (1969) study of Manchester councillors came to the same conclusion that very few councillors exhibit any great interest in policy making and only seventeen per cent reported having any specific policy goal they hoped to accomplish, and only fourteen per cent mentioned participation in policy making as very important to them. The great satisfaction for most of them was in helping

constituents on a fairly direct and personal basis. This of course, as
Jones (1973) points out, contrasts very sharply with the role of
councillors as seen by the Maud Committee which conceived of them
as determining broad policy and objectives. In this respect the Bains
Report is more realistic in recognizing the diversity of roles
councillors may want to play*.

This diversity of roles is well illustrated by Lewis Corina's (1974)
study of Halifax councillors. Taking the role of party member he
finds it useful to introduce no less than five sub-sets. The 'ideologist'
who tended to express strong convictions which when they ran
counter to those of other members, including their own party, were
pursued to the point of open and uncompromising opposition. His
loyalty to party was based on the often vain hope of 'educating' it to
accept his principles. By contrast the 'party politician's' loyalty to his
party was based on his belief in the necessity of cohesion to achieve
certain long term goals. The 'partyist's' loyalty to party is an end in
itself. He sees the party as determining for him his voting behaviour,
is intolerant of internal disputes and often judges the merits of issues
on the basis of whether they originated in his party or not. The
'associate', whilst a party member does not fully identify with his
party and his membership is often no more than an electoral
necessity. The 'politico-administrators' are the most influential
people on the council and hold most of the key positions. Many have
served for long periods and are conditioned to the system. They are
willing to shoulder responsibility and devote a considerable amount
of their time to the work. They enjoy particularly close relations with
officers and share with them a commitment to 'making the authority
work well as a system for providing social services'. This last group
was numerically quite small and reminds us again of the point that
only a small number of members adopt policy making roles.

---

*Bains distinguishes five tasks — broad policy makers, welfare activities, management
along commercial lines, controlling expenditure and serving the community at large.
Helco distinguishes three — committee member, constituency representative and
party activist.
Jones suggests a tripology of broad policy maker, specialized policy maker and
representative and impressionalistically estimates the latter comprise 75 per cent and
the former 5 per cent and 20 per cent of councillors respectively.
Self (1971) distinguishes between five roles, policy maker and resource allocator,
reviewer of the exercize of official discretion, welfare role, spokesman for consumers
of particular services and party role.

Lee's (1963, p.154) study of Cheshire suggests an inner ring of senior councillors and chief officers dominating decision making even to the extent that 'certain facts, such as the precise distribution of grammar school places, were not available even to all members of the Education Committee'. Lee's distinction between 'ministerialists' and other councillors corresponds broadly to the distinction between Cabinet members and backbenchers in central government, with the former largely monopolizing policy making. Studies of political leadership at the local level suggest a link between leadership and a more or less full-time commitment to the job. Jones (1973, p.10) taking Herbert Morrison as an archetype, writes 'Much of Morrison's success came from his obsession with politics. He had no other interests. Politics dominated his whole life. Family and friends were sacrificed to his overriding political involvement. The lesson is that to be a success in politics requires a commitment to political activity that few are able to make'. Case studies of comprehensive reorganization confirm the view that decision making tends to be in the hands of very few people. Parkinson (1972) found that only ten per cent of members felt that the individual councillor had any contribution to make to policy making. Experience of service on the education committee may not have done very much to effect their views on educational policy but it had affected their views of the decision making process. This they now saw as more problematic than they had initially imagined and this in turn reduced their confidence in what they, as individuals, could achieve. In West Ham, Pescheck (1972, p.67) concluded 'both the present Chairman of the Education Committee and the Chief Education Officer are strong personalities and are at the core of decision making. Perhaps not more than two or three other Councillors have any real influence'. Rigby (1975) in Crawley also attributes the pressure for reorganization to one or two councillors arguing that the majority were 'not equipped by their backgrounds or interests to understand the implications and complexities of educational provision'. In effect all welcomed the social prestige of being councillors but few were willing to work hard mastering the complexities of policy. Similarly, Saran (1968) is of the opinion that over the twenty year period she studied no more than half a dozen councillors in each party had much direct say on policy and in both parties there was one person who probably had the main say over the whole period. One of the explanations given being that councillors in general knew very little about education and within each party a small number of 'experts' made all the running. It was these who had close relations with officers and access to information. A major factor again was the availability of time and it is worth noting that of the seven Chairmen of the Education Committee five were retired and the other two teachers in their late fifties who probably also had more than average 'free' time available to them. Certainly the importance of education committee chairmen is considerable compared to that of other members.

A study of Leeds (Fenwicke and Woodthorpe, 1980) showed how an experienced education chairman was able to move his fellow Tories to the point where they accepted his reorganization proposals and where he managed for much of the time to act with considerable independence. A number of factors explain his success in doing so. His party had been out of office for fourteen years and the members were relatively inexperienced with nearly three quarters of them having been councillors for less than four years. By contrast the education chairman had been on the council over twenty years having been education chairman in the previous Tory administration and its chief education spokesman since. Secondly, for much of the time he managed to conceal from his colleagues just how fully comprehensive his proposals were. Finally there was a general willingness within the party to accept strong leadership and the concentration of power in relatively few hands.

Obviously chairmen constitute a major group within the council hierarchy given the centrality of the committee system in English local government. The chairman's role is not a prescribed one and it has evolved according to the needs of particular committees and departments and the qualities of the individuals chosen to fill it. Formally, chairmen have no greater powers than any other members but in practice exert an influence far greater than the average member. This comes as a result of many factors. Their close relationship with the chief officers tends to make them better informed than most members. In addition they will probably be fairly experienced and senior members of the council and of their party. They are in a strong position to determine the structure and length of committee discussions. Quite often they have delegated powers to act on behalf of their committee between meetings. They will represent their committee in council and party meetings and before the policy and resources committee. They are the spokesmen, watchdogs and interpreters of party policy within education committee and in their relations with chief officers. As Birley comments (1970, p.130): 'The power of a determined, ambitious and skilful chairman is very considerable indeed'. The actual role of chairmen depends on the personality, ability, experience, energy and role conception of the individual. Some chairmen see their role as dominant in policy initiation while others would see this as a usurpation of their committee's powers. Also relevant would be the characteristics of fellow committee members and chief officers. Committee chairmen interviewed by Jennings (1977) were almost unanimous in agreeing that very few members contributed policy alternatives and attributed this to lack of time and knowledge. Dearlove (1976, p.132) commented on the relationship between chairmen and committee members concluding:

> In hard reality they lack the capacity to appoint or dismiss the chairman, and it is difficult for them to defy the chairman's lead in committee or party meeting, or to refuse to endorse the decisions which the chairman makes in the name of the council between meetings.

And yet the influence of chairmen is linked to the nature of party control exercised by the majority party and the relations between the chairmen and party leaders. Jennings (Ibid) argues that the proposals of an informed and dependable chairman are nearly always accepted by the majority group. At the same time chairmen whose ideas of how to achieve party objectives are seen as not going far or fast enough may find themselves being instructed by group leaders. This seems more likely in the case of Labour controlled councils given that party's greater emphasis on pursuing defined objectives and checking proposals for congruence with those. In addition party leaders may use the policy and resources committee as a means of subjecting chairmen's proposals to financial scrutiny. This is particularly likely where the role of this committee is seen as distinct from that of the party group and where the autonomy of the education committee is subject to challenge. The net result being that education chairmen are being increasingly required to justify their proposals and account for their use of funds. Party leaders are more and more concerned with controlling the financial demands of an enormously expensive service. Naturally this is especially the case at a time of economic stringency and when the claims of education compared with other services are seen as less paramount than in the past.

In terms of Boaden's (1971) model of the local political system councillors could be expected to exercize considerable collective impact. Boaden's model suggests that the activity in any service will depend on the needs of the area, the disposition of the authority in providing that service, and on the availability of resources to finance the service. Disposition can be seen as a key factor relating the other two. The first dimension of disposition is in regard to what constitutes desirable standards and scale of provision. The second is concerned with disposition towards the needs of particular groups within the community such as the young and the old. The third concerns the desirability and legitimacy of government action to meet perceived needs. Needs, in other words, only become operational politically when they are perceived as such by decision makers who are also sympathetic to those involved and who see them as legitimate claimants for authority support. Disposition also affects what decision makers see as reasonable levels of public expenditure and their willingness to increase the availability of resources. Donnison *et al.* (1975) define elected members as 'resource controllers' and although given a degree of local dependence on central finance their control is not complete, variations in local expenditure by authority are sufficient to suggest the title is not inappropriate.

Councillors are the formal decision makers in the local government system. Within the constraints imposed by the central government they are the group which has the power to make or veto all important decisions. It has been traditional in political science to counter the reality of such statements by stressing the environmental constraints imposed on formal decision makers and the limited room for manoeuvre thus available to them. These constraints are usually characterized as electoral pressures, the existence of powerful pressure groups and socio-economic variables. Systems theory, with its view of policy making as a conversion process of inputs into outputs has encouraged this view of formal decision makers seeing them very much as the victims of a system over which they have very limited control. Obviously local councillors must be to a degree responsive to their environment, however there is a danger that in stressing the external constraints the real freedom of choice available to them is ignored. We have already argued against the view which sees local authorities merely as agents of the central government. The subsequent discussion of the roles of parents and electors suggests their impact is not great. Although teachers, for reasons discussed, have a greater influence the evidence does not support the idea of them as an effective initiating group. Thus the relative scarcity of active groups in the field, the frequent lack of any real conflict, the fact that parents were often badly if at all organized and teachers divided and consulted often late in the day, prevents the reorganization of secondary education being explained wholly in terms of a pressure group model. Rather our evidence suggests that it was the local authority which was often the prime initiator and developer of policies. It further suggests that it was a fairly small group of councillors in the majority party who typically exercized real decision making power. However, before supporting such a conclusion we need to examine an alternative explanation and that is that the real power lies more with officers than members.

Officers and members

The relationship between officials and elected representatives is a major issue in the literature of public administration. This is particularly true at the level of central government where a growing, if somewhat inconclusive, literature exists. There is no doubt that this is an enormously difficult area to research. Many of the accounts of the relationships are written by the participants themselves. As the authors of one of the best studies (Helco and Wildavsky, 1974, p.xix) of the inner workings of British central government write, 'The political administrative culture of British central government is a shadowy realm usually left to chance observations in politicians' memoirs or civil servant valedictories'. This raises a number of problems. There may well be a tendency to describe the relationship in terms of the usual cliches neither side being willing to suggest things were other than they should have been. Apart from this there is the question of how representative are those who put their experiences into print. For example, it is plausible to imagine the three retired or about to retire Chief Education Officers (CEOs) interviewed by Kogan (1973) were in many respects untypical of their counterparts. Even so, Kogan was fortunate to be able to arrange such interviews and most academics find their experience more like that of the researcher who received from the civil service 'nothing but courtesy'. As Newton (1976, p.146) comments in his study of Birmingham '. . . there is little doubt that in local as in central government the theme of bureaucratic control is as crucially important as it is difficult to study. In fact getting any quantity of hard and reliable information is like trying to get blood out of red tape'. A major shortcoming of an otherwise excellent study (Dearlove, 1973, p229) of local policy making is its complete failure to study the part played by officers. 'Many of the officers were interviewed but it proved impossible to break through the cultural cliche that they were simply servants advising the all powerful policy making councillors whose decisions they readily implemented.' Similarly, Regan's (1977) study completely fails to discuss the relationship between Chief Education Officers and members and, indeed, manages to ignore the political dimension in education almost completely. Even Birley (1970) himself once a deputy CEO, contributes very little to our understanding of this relationship.

Various attempts over time have been made to distinguish between the roles of officers and members. Some of these have had strong prescriptive overtones arguing that a clearer understanding of the 'proper' roles of each side would contribute greatly to the efficiency of local government. The traditional distinction has focussed on the dividing line between administration and policy with the former reserved for officers and the latter for members. Thus one Clerk in evidence to the Maud Committee (1967) wrote:

> In any cases where officials have tried to interfere with policy, I have rapped them firmly over the knuckles. Conversely and somewhat more violently if necessary, any member of the council who showed a tendency to interfere with administration was very firmly handled.

But most commentators agree that the dividing line has proved more elusive than this statement suggests as policy decisions shade imperceptibly into administrative decisions.

Furthermore, if even such a line could be drawn it would not serve as a useful division. Policy requires the contribution of officers and administration the oversight of members. The Maud Committee (1967) exploded the myth of policy being a matter solely for elected members and administration for officers. The Bains Committee (1972) argued that neither group can regard any area of an authorities' work as exclusively theirs. Members have a legitimate interest in the day to day administration of cases involving their constituents. Officers have a role to play in the stimulation and formulation of policy and in providing members with the necessary advice and evaluation to enable them to make decisions. The Bains Report supports a view of the management process which characterizes it as a scale with the setting of objectives at one end moving through the designing of plans and onto the detailed execution at the other end. In this context one moves from member control and officer advice at the objective end through to officer control and member advice at the execution end. This is a reasonable picture provided one doesn't assume that the management process can be divided into two watertight halves, thus resurrecting the false dichotomy between policy and administration. Also providing one realizes that in the final analysis member control and intervention cannot be precluded from any area given that any area can become political. Furthermore, it must be remembered that viewpoints expressed in both the Maud and Bains Reports are largely at the prescriptive level and the reality within local authorities may be very different and certainly not uniform between authorities. Such distinctions as between new and routine, major and minor, means and ends, unprogrammed and programmed, political and non-political, value and facts, controversial and non-controversial decisions are at best generalizations for what are infinitely variable sets of relationships.

According to traditional democratic theory the bureaucracy is not expected to interfere in the determination of policy but confines itself to the application of pre-determined policy. Most writers have been at pains to expose the unreality of this viewpoint. Thus Weber (1947) comments 'control of existing bureaucratic machinery is possible only in a very limited degree to persons who are not technical specialists. Generally speaking the trained permanent official is more likely to get his way in the long run than his nominal superior ... who is not a specialist'. Some writers go as far as to suggest that reality is largely a reversal of the formal constitutional position. Lee (1963, p.214) in Cheshire found Chief Officers so central to policy making that he describes the system of local government in that area as 'a body of professional people, placed together in a large office at County Hall, who can call upon the services of representatives throughout the area which they administer'. The Education Committee is described as having 'little choice but to accept the recommendations made by its officers'. Heclo (1969) also argues that the constitutional position is reversed to the extent that the official is the policy maker and the members carry out routine administration in committees.

Nor are there any shortages of explanations for such a state of affairs. The major source of official power is councillor dependence on them. There is an obvious sense in which they depend on them for the day to day running of departments but more significant is dependence on them for policy advice. Increasingly policy making is seen to be a complex process moving through a series of stages over time. These stages have been formulated by different writers in various ways but usually involve problem identification, goal setting, search activity and evaluation of alternatives, consultation and authorization. This is obviously a very complex and time-consuming process and almost inevitably has to be largely undertaken by officials. As Neville Johnson (1965, p.287) puts it 'when we look at policy making as fact finding, analysis and recommendations then it is officials who dominate and will continue to do so'.

Chief Education Officers

Not only does the CEO have at his disposal substantial sources of information and administrative experience, he also mediates between his authority and the DES and with local interest groups especially the teachers. He is the head of his department and his subordinates depend on him in matters of promotion, recommendation and transfer. He is in a nearly monopolistic position regarding the formal channels of communication. He approves the drafting of agendas and minutes of committees and sub-committees. It is at his level that a good deal of what March and Simon (1958) term 'absorption of uncertainty' in the lines of communication to committees and the council takes place. Most requests, regulations and data are chanelled through him and information access and control must be regarded at a major power resource (Pettigrew, 1972). Inherent in the position of 'information gatekeeper' is the potential not only to control the flow of information to members but also to collect, combine and reformulate information. He has the necessary resources to formulate policies in detail and assess their feasibility. As

Hill (1972, p.225) comments, 'The professional's strength particularly lies in his ability to invest his views in a certain scientific or quasi-scientific rationality, to draw from 'facts' to support his viewpoint'. His knowledge of education both at the national and local levels will almost certainly exceed that of members. He is more likely to have close contacts with CEOs in other authorities and his counterparts at the DES. Certainly there are well known cases such as Clegg in the West Riding and Mason in Leicestershire where the CEO could reasonably be regarded as the author of secondary reorganization.

Of course, officers who have been closely involved in the development of educational arrangements may well, as a result, have personal and professional stakes in their continuation. At the same time, they are likely to be aware of shortcomings in the system, of trends in educational thinking and see their role as including innovation. Kogan's (1973) CEOs certainly saw themselves as responsible for instigating changes within the system. Several of the case studies show CEOs own thinking on secondary reorganization changed over time in the direction of being more sympathetic to it. In Bath (White, 1974) the CEOs opposition to reorganization was a major constraint but by the late 1960s he had become increasingly disturbed by the administrative and planning problems caused by continuing uncertainty. As a result, instead of pressing on the authority, as previously, the objections of teachers he now pressed the dangers of delay. This episode illustrates neatly the powers of the CEO as an information gatekeeper. It also illustrates the role of administrative feedback in that officers as administrators may be more aware of the need to introduce changes to deal with deficiences in existing policy.

Thus Donnison *et al.* (1975) argues that it is the providers of services, the officers, who usually initiate changes. This they argue is particularly true when the providers are trained, skilled, given high discretion and operate services which depend more on their direct contact with clients than costly capital investments or cash payments. Donnison agrees that to the extent innovation depends on additional resources the providers also need the support of members as resource controllers. However, in secondary reorganization it was less the need for additional resources which involved members but more the highly political nature of the issue itself. This is Saran's (1973) conclusion, namely, that officers initiate changes only in those areas which have not been seen to be politically sensitive. This brings us to a crucial point in any consideration of the roles of officers and members. This is that such an exercize is meaningless unless consideration is given to the nature of the particular issues under review as the roles of both sides are almost infinitely variable. When the issue is seen as largely non-political officers may dominate the entire process of policy initiation, authorization and implementation while where the issue is political members will want to retain a say even in the smallest detail of administration. Thus Saran shows how whereas in the 1940s selection processes were a non-political issue left wholly to officers to determine this ceased to be true in the 1950's as such processes became the subject of public controversy.

In this context the influence of party on the relationship is most significant. The comment of Dan Cook, one of the CEOs interviewed by Kogan (1973), that councillors did not have great impact on policy making may well be in part a reflection of the fact that his authority did not run on strict party lines. Officers are likely to find it easier to control decision making when faced with an array of individuals and independents rather than organized and disciplined parties. Even in party authorities much will depend on the nature of the party system. Thus, in West Ham (Peschech *et al.,* 1966) despite a permanent Labour majority the lack of political opposition and vigorous interest groups led to something of a vacuum which was filled by the CEO as the major innovatory force. Likewise in Reading (Pescheck, ibid) the majority party was bereft of any real interest in education and innovative leadership passed into the hands of the CEO. In Darlington the CEO's role in drawing up a scheme was so prominent that it was named after him while the opposition Conservative party complained bitterly that it was 'the view of one man and one man alone'. (Batley *et al.,* 1970, p.47).

On the other hand, where a party comes to power with an educational policy of its own, officers tend to loose the initiative and have to produce plans even for policies they would not themselves put forward. This certainly is Saran's conclusion in Middlesex and is reflected elsewhere. In Gateshead (Batley, ibid) a powerful disciplined Labour Party in more or less continuous office was able to establish a situation where the CEO was faced with firm policy decisions which he was left to develop into administratively workable schemes. Jones (1969) has shown how the expansion of party politics in Wolverhampton served to reduce the powers of officers. In the earlier years neither Conservative nor Liberal parties had any clear municipal programmes to implement and there was ample scope for chief officers to intervene with ideas of their own. With the growth of parties that role was increasingly seen as belonging to the party group. The significance of political will is central. For example, in Liverpool (Parkinson, 1972) in the absence of such a will it was possible for the CEO to depress demands for reorganization but once the issue caught the imagination of the parties they took control of decision making and the CEO lost command of events.

The significance of party is clearly brought out in a comparative study of Oxford City and Oxfordshire County (Rhodes, 1974). In the former, attempts at reorganization were dominated by the political parties and officers were limited to providing members with information rather than taking the initiative. Party groups were highly developed and very significant as initiators and coordinators of policy. By contrast in Oxfordshire the parties did not take a prominent role and the initiative throughout lay with the CEO. Party groups were only weakly developed and not organized to exert concerted pressure on officers. Thus the CEO was able to implement wide ranging reforms without any council opposition and negotiating directly with various groups winning support for his policies and thus legitimizing his actions. Similarly a comparative study of reorganization in four LEAs in the Sheffield area (Fearn, 1977) shows the role of the CEO related to the nature of the party system. Where the parties are well organized and the majority party enjoys prolonged tenure of office the CEO's role is a largely subordinate one. In authorities where the parties are less organized and secure, CEOs play a greater role though in no case did they emerge as major initiators of change.

Neve (1977) on the basis of interviews with forty CEOs and an equal number of deputies concludes that instances where officers dominate educational policy making are few especially in large urban authorities with highly developed party systems. He sees their role in such situations more as 'facilitators', 'catalysts', reconciling different interests, bargaining and coalition building. David (1977) also on the basis of interviews with large numbers of officers identifies what she terms a 'conciliator' role whereby officers test policy options according to the amount of political support they attract. This brokerage role is contrasted with the 'educator' style where options derive from and are tested against educational considerations with the emphasis on the CEO's function as innovator and educational leader. Such differences are largely related to the personality of individual CEOs and in some instances a change in personnel led to an abrupt change in style. Thus in one northern LEA 'Brownborough' an 'educator' CEO who exerted considerable influence over policy died and was replaced by his deputy who followed a 'conciliator' style. David (ibid), p.87) describes the changes as follows:

> The early work of the education officers was inspired by educational motives. Later it can best be seen as a continuous process of amending, adapting and responding to the wishes of pressure groups. Their recent work was conciliatory. The officers felt that the constraints were inevitable but some were clearly self-imposed . . . Not surprisingly, their educational objectives, never clearly articulated after 1965 were lost in a sea of opinion from the various participants at both central and local level.

The conciliator's role proved the commoner and it is arguable that as education becomes increasingly subject to constraints and counter pressures officers' roles as innovators may become secondary to that of creating alliances to protect education's interests in an increasingly hostile environment. In such circumstances officers have little option but to tailor their educational advice to the restraints imposed by the economic and political climate, acting as political filters assessing information and ideas in terms of their political as well as educational feasability.

In the discussion of the impact of party on officer-member relations Hill (1972) makes a valuable distinction between two styles of politics, ideological and administrative politics*. Ideological politics typically occurs where there is a fully fledged, competitive and disciplined party system. Patronage will be distributed on party lines, an effective whip and caucus system will operate and a one party cabinet system will cut across the committee system. To the extent such party meetings exclude officers and determine policy on party lines, the influence of officers is accordingly reduced. Also in

---

*Hill also distinguishes a third category, bargaining politics, but plausibly argues that this is not at all common in English local government but more useful as a description of American local government.

such a situation the relationship between members and officers is more clear-cut with officers being in less doubt as to what policy is to be and what is politically possible and what is not. In administrative politics administrators dominate the decision making process and members are treated either as representatives of the general public or of particular interest groups. Their views will be taken into account and some of them may be co-opted primarily as individuals rather than representatives into the policy making process. But officers will regard members as one among many sources of public opinion rather than as the single voice of the public will. This style of politics is reinforced to the extent that councillors prefer to concentrate on routine rather than policy issues. Administrative politics is generally found on councils where there is an absence of party groups capable of giving some political control over policy and acting in a unified manner. In the absence of such groups thinking about future policy passes largely into the hands of the permanent officials who may or may not be innovative. As Hill puts it (ibid, p.234):

> Administrative politics may involve situations in which administrators have considerable freedom to innovate, particularly where they are protected from the public by a moribund political system. They may therefore secure the autonomy to put in practice their ideals and commitments, and it is for this reason that one finds occasionally in Britain striking innovations stemming from local authorities in which politicians play a minor part.

A few instances can be found where this pattern seems to have prevailed but overall CEO autonomy is more the exception than the rule. It may also be argued that in some of the earlier cases of reorganization such as Leicestershire and Coventry where the role of the CEO was dominant this was due in part to reorganization being at that time less party political. When subsequently it became an increasingly partisan issue the centre for initiative moved from officers to party groups. Richard Rose (1969) has argued that the effectiveness of elected representatives in achieving operational control of government depends on a number of factors. First, the fact of control being centred in a single party which enjoys an overall majority. Secondly, that such a party will have formulated policy in terms of what it wants to do. Thirdly, that there must be high priority given to carrying out these policies even in the face of difficulties.

Fourthly, that elected representatives have the necessary skills to control large bureaucratic organizations. Although these factors were formulated in the context of national government the analysis is not without relevance to local government.

Changes in local government leading to increased party influence on decision making make it more likely that some of these criteria will be met. There is evidence to suggest a possible difference between the two major parties. For example, Saran (1973, p.253) commenting on reorganization in Middlesex points out:

> Labour leaders had a clear line to follow, namely to start comprehensive schools and abolish selection, and, therefore, kept the initiative in their own hands. Conservatives on the other hand, were united in opposition to these changes, but lacked positive alternatives of their own. They, therefore, relied in the main on officers for policy proposals.

Similarly in a wider ranging study Jennings (1977, p.140) discerned differences between the parties in terms of the importance attached to the achievement of clearly defined party goals.

> Every Labour leader that was questioned expressed the notion of party aims and the responsibility of the party for achieving particular outcomes. One summed it up as follows, "We don't soft pedal our socialism — if we decide we have an aim or an idea of how something should be done we say so". By contrast no Conservative leader mentioned party goals or responsibility as ends in themselves.

Whatever the party's aims and aspirations there are those who doubt whether members have the necessary skills to actually determine policy decisions. The growing complexity of policy issues is often cited as explanation of increased official power. The Maud Committee (1967) stated that many Chief Officers thought members were unable to grasp issues of any complexity. There was much evidence from Chief Officers that over the years many spheres of local government had become so highly technical that its intricacies were, in large measure, incomprehensible to the layman. Parkinson (1972) found support for the idea that members often have difficulty in absorbing all the information they are supplied with by officers and about a half of them felt disadvantaged by their lack of expertise, information and time compared with officers. All three of Kogan's

(1973) CEOs emphasized the difficulties lay councillors experience in dealing with issues facing the education service.

At the same time it is possible to overdo this picture of the incompetent and part-time member versus the expert and experienced officer. Councils include a wide range of competent professional people, especially if cooptees are included, while many councillors, especially leading members, manage by a variety of means to spend large amounts of time on council business, often specializing in particular spheres. There are members whose experience in their particular authority is greater than most officers and by no means all of them are so immersed in administrative detail that they leave policy issues to officers. Newton in his study of Birmingham (1976) notes a variety of different member-officer relationships and argues that those members who occupy the important positions as chairmen or group leaders are most likely to want to be 'in absolute control of policy'. His general conclusion being 'there is good hard evidence in this study to show that much of the current literature on officer-member relations over-emphasizes the power of officers and under-emphasizes that of members' (ibid, p.164). In discussing officer-member relations it is important to distinguish between the influence of front benchers and back benchers. Recent internal changes such as the creation of policy committees and officer management groups have reinforced the tendency to concentrate power in fewer and fewer hands. Several of the studies point to the existence of small numbers of 'experts' on education who set the pace and through regular contacts with officers are well informed and influential in persuading fellow members to follow their lead. Such 'experts' are usually the most senior members both in terms of position and years of service. Their experience on the council may well extend over twenty or more years. They may spend anything up to a hundred hours a week on council business and have a detailed knowledge of the locality and educational issues. The division between this group and the younger, less experienced and committed members seems to be widening as various organizational reforms lead to the creation and strengthening of Cabinet systems within local authorities.

Whatever their own views there is no evidence in any of these studies of officers deliberately obstructing or failing to comply with LEAs decisions. Saran (1973) notes, for example, that although

officers were personally opposed to Labour's early attempts in
Middlesex to introduce comprehensive education and later to modify
11+ procedures officers loyally addressed public meetings and
cooperated with teachers in designing new procedures. Like their
counterparts in Whitehall they adhere to a tradition of political
neutrality and accept the need to read their masters' political minds
when tendering advice. At the same time this does not prevent them
from attempting to influence the ways those minds operate — in
Self's (1972) teminology they are more political chameleons than
political eunuchs. Such attempts were by no means always successful.
Middlesex's Labour councillors remained unmoved by the CEO's
attempt to allow grammar schools to opt out of the comprehensive
plan. On the other hand, Southampton's Chief Education Officer was
the key influence in persuading the newly elected Conservative
Council not to abandon the comprehsive scheme just drawn up by the
previous Labour Council (White, 1974). His ability to do this was
linked to the fact that the Conservatives had been in opposition for
fourteen years and lacked the confidence and experience to challenge
the powerful case put forward by the CEO who was a determined
supporter of the comprehensive idea. A similar story could be told in
Darlington (Batley, 1970) where the CEO convinced the new
Conservative Council that their alternative plan was simply
unworkable. But it would be wrong to assume that all CEOs were
either strongly for or against reorganization and some took the role
of neutral policy advisers. Lewin (1969) comments that, CEOs in
Outer London 'have been singularly reluctant to put their general
educational thoughts on reorganization onto paper' and the CEO in
Merton 'at no stage attempted to persuade the Council of the
advantages of one policy but played more the role of a technical
adviser on the sidelines laying out alternative schemes. Similarly in
Birmingham (Isaac-Henry, 1970) the CEO played a largely
'spectator' role not imposing his personal views on the education
committee but moving in whatever direction the majority party
intimated. A divided Labour group, an education committee
weakened by frequent changes of chairman and lack of lead from the
CEO contributed to delay reorganization. When in 1965 a plan was
agreed it was done so by a majority of one and overthrown within
months when the Tories took control of the council. Again in
Bradford (Dark, 1967) where the Labour group was also strongly

divided the CEO made no attempt to resolve the differences and played a largely passive role throughout.

The trials and tribulations of even a determined CEO are well illustrated in the case of Croydon (Turnbull, 1969). Here the CEO carefully prepared his ground by the collection of local data to prove conclusively the weaknesses of Croydon's selective system in terms of unreliable selection and wastage of grammar school places. He even called in outside experts to support him — with mixed results! He had furthermore a passionate interest in his junior college scheme. Despite all this the scheme was not accepted. In Manchester (Stern, 1971) the CEO attempted to play a moderating role arguing for gradual and experimental changes only. In drawing up such a scheme he failed to discuss it with his chairman taking the view that his function as CEO was to tender advice regardless of likely party reaction. Not surprisingly reaction to the scheme was hostile and led to a deterioration of relations between him and the Labour group. The final scheme was carried against his advice and in the face of persistent teacher and parent opposition.

Of all the cliches used to describe the relationship the commonest is that of partnership. I have already argued that as a descripton of central-local relations the term is misleading and this is also my contention here. It is a concept which conceals more than it reveals and is a gross over-simplification of what is a highly complex and variable relationship. The conclusion that 'the relationship between politicians and administrators in the formation of policy was a partnership' really tells us very little. Was it a partnership of equals, if not what were the bases and consequences of the inequalities, what was distinctive about each partner's contribution, how did the partnership alter over time and by issue, what were the strains in the partnership and how were these resolved? Such questions are, of course, easier to ask than to answer but to assume that a catch-phrase such as partnership is a sufficient answer is patently false. it is particularly misleading to use it to describe relationships which vary so much as between different authorities.

The study of the relationship between officers and members is a frustrating one. Partly because of the difficulties of gaining access to the 'facts', partly because of the immense variability of the relationship and partly because of the difficulties of adequately characterizing such a subtle and complex set of relationships. It is not, therefore, altogether surprising that writers often fall back on such convenient phrases as partnership — phrases which, however, reveal more our ignorance than our understanding of this crucial relationship.

Chapter Seven

Conclusions and Prospects

The purpose of this concluding chapter is not to attempt a summary of the preceding chapters. Each chapter has already included its own conclusions and whatever broad conclusions are made here must be balanced by the more detailed discussion in the individual chapters. My main concern here is rather to look to the future of studies in local policy making outlining possible areas for future research and commenting on issues of methodology.

The Central Government

The study of the relations between central and local government has given growing support for the view that local authorities are more than mere administrative appendages of the central government. The attack on that traditional perspective has tended to rely on statistical studies showing variations in expenditure patterns between local authorities. The literature on secondary reorganization has served to focus attention on the individual responses of particular LEAs to government pressures. It has shown two main things. Firstly, that policy initiatives do not necessarily originate from the centre. In fact, a number of LEAs had either reorganized or were seriously considering doing so well before the central government was committed to such a course of action. Indeed until 1965, the role of the central government whether Labour or Conservative controlled, was usually to inhibit and delay local initiative in this area. Secondly, when the centre did take the initiative the response of individual LEAs varied considerably. Undoubtedly, the great majority fell into line fairly quickly but much depended on their party composition and particular circumstances and personalities. In some cases, central pressure served as a catalyst strengthening the arm of those, officers, members, teachers and parents, wishing to see change. In others it had the reverse effect of stimulating opposition by making the issue clearly one of party politics. In these latter circumstances the weakness of DES's position was exposed and the limitations of central 'control' when faced with hostile and determined LEAs made apparent. The nature of central government mechanisms have always been such as to make it easier to prevent rather than to promote changes at the local level. In the final analysis, given our system of government, a central authority able and willing to legislate and determined to get its own way will eventually succeed in doing so. But given the traditions of that system the central authority feels obliged to proceed diplomatically and with care in its dealing with large and powerful LEAs. By and large the DES prefers to avoid wherever possible confrontations. It prefers exercizing influence rather than control and using persuasion rather than force. Terms such as regulation and control are less appropriate than bargaining and consultation.

It was the role of pioneering LEAs and small numbers of teachers and social scientists to put the case for comprehensive schooling onto the political agenda. They were faced with considerable obstacles including opposition from within both major parties both nationally and locally, suspicion and divisions within parental and teacher opinions, the heritage of established schools and traditions, the cost and complexity of reorganization and the natural caution and inertia of administrators both in the Ministry and locally. The process was incremental with changes slow and usually piecemeal. The forces opposed to sudden alterations and operating to preserve elements of the status quo exercized a powerful role. Parent groups fighting to preserve individual grammar schools, teachers concerned about their conditions of service and career prospects, older councillors intent on defending systems of which they had often been the major architects, Conservative councils opposed to direction by a Labour government, CEOs anxious to moderate the pace of change and urging limited experiments. Remembering the extent of the consensus which surrounded the selective system in the post war years such resistance to its rejection is not surprising. Even when that consensus began to break down it was not immediately replaced by a new consensus and there was a considerable period of uncertainty, caution and division. During this time the forces of change gathered strength but the initial unwillingness of Labour governments to do other than proceed by persuasion and the changing fortunes of the parties both nationally and locally all served to slow down the rate of change.

The Labour government, despite its commitment to reorganization, only slowly and reluctantly introduced legislation to force LEAs to go comprehensive. Considerable leeway was allowed local authorities in drawing up their plans and the DES was throughout very conscious of local conditions and resources. It is difficult to see Labour governments as having introduced hasty, doctrinaire and uniform changes as some of their opponents claimed. Conservative governments gave LEAs a greater independence in determining their systems of secondary education. In doing so and in criticizing Labour's more centralized approach they made political capital out of their supposed regard for local autonomy. In reality, as recent events suggest, the Conservatives can hardly be portrayed as defenders of local independence and their motives were more to safeguard existing grammar schools. A policy of laissez-faire put the onus for change on the LEAs while still preserving for the central government the power to block such changes as they disapproved of. It enabled authorities which wanted to preserve their selective system to do so while those wanting to change theirs might find the government rejecting those parts of their proposal which entailed the abolition of prestigious grammar schools.

However, the pace of change was not wholly dependent on the attitudes of the central government. Between 1970 and 1974 Margaret Thatcher presided over the demise of more grammar schools than any previous Minister of Education. Indeed throughout the period since 1965, despite changes of government, the speed of reorganization has remained surprisingly constant. The causes of educational change are never wholly political. The opinions of educationalists, the attitudes of the teaching profession and the aspirations of parents all played a part. Economic arguments such as the need to rationalize resources in rural areas or situations of falling numbers of children have also encouraged the creation of comprehensive schools. Certainly much of the initiative for change lay with the LEAs rather than the central authorities. It was individual LEAs which in the face of central discouragement pioneered the creation of comprehensives in the forties and fifties. When national government introduced its own plans in the mid sixties it drew heavily on the experience of those authorities.

Certainly the relationship between central and local government has not been a static one. In recent years it has been largely overshadowed by economic factors. The decline in the economy has led to concerted efforts by central government to curb the scale of public expenditure. Local authority expenditure having grown more rapidly than other areas has received particular attention in this respect. The imposition of cash limits, sharp limitations in the size of the rate support grant and pressures to bring spending under greater control have all meant increased central control. The Conservative government elected in 1979 has announced its intention to take this control still further. Most drastically it is proposing to replace the present rate support grant by a unitary grant. Such a grant would mean the central government assessing how much it believes each local authority should spend. It will also set standard approved rate levels for local authorities. On the basis of these figures the government will then determine how much of the total cost it will meet. Local authorities spending more than the government deems necessary will find the government reducing its share of the total cost. In addition the government intends imposing tighter controls on the total of capital spending by individual authorities. Not surprisingly the local authority associations have expressed grave apprehension seeing these moves as marking a major change in central-local relations. It remains to be seen to what extent the government will take account of these apprehensions.

Undoubtedly such research as we have, and notably that of Griffith (1966) has increased considerably our understanding of central local relations. In particular, earlier views of central domination have now largely been rejected as misleading. Nevertheless this remains an area where much research still has to be done. At the level of policy making we need to know much more about the ways and extent to which local authorities, as through their professional associations and party links, influence central government policy. Similarly, we need to examine the effects of central pressures on local policy making. It is likely that each side will frame policies in the light of anticipated reactions by the other but the exact nature and extent of this reciprocal relationship is inadequately understood.

At the level of policy implementation we need to know not only the mechanisms of central direction but also the conditions in which they are invoked and the various responses of local authorities. It is certain that central government does not respond uniformly towards all local authorities any more than they act uniformly towards the centre. Neither side is monolithic. Griffith (Ibid) has clearly shown various central departments react in different ways towards local authorities. Some departments being more interventionist than others and much hinging on traditions, powers and the political importance attached to different services. But less frequently is the point made that local authorities also differ in their reactions to central control. While some are docile others are skilfull in using their various resources, financial, legal and political, to subvert intervention of which they disapprove. We need to know far more about the factors affecting the reactions of individual authorities to central departments and the nature of the bargaining and interaction which results.

As has been argued the relationship is far from a static one and some of the earlier work including Griffith's is now very dated. It may well be that we are entering an era of increasing central control and where studies of local policy making will need to take greater account of prevailing national policies and the state of the national economy. Local authorities never have been isolated islands and analysis of their political processes must be firmly grounded in a consideration of the wider economic and political environment of which they are a part.

Parents and Teachers

The literature of public policy making usually stresses the influence of voter demands and pressure group activity on policy. Governments, central and local, are often conceived of as weak bodies facing a strong environment of external demands and constraints. As Eckstein (1962) has characterized it, the formal decision makers simply serve as cash registers ringing up claims and debits as these are entered by parties, pressure groups and all others able to mobilize support. Local authorities in particular, are often attributed with the virtue of being highly vulnerable and receptive to such demands. Despite the obviously important and controversial nature of secondary reorganization there is little in these case studies to sustain such a viewpoint.

Elections for a variety of reasons are shown to be an inadequate device for either determining or holding to account those who do determine local policies. Not surprisingly, parents have followed the example of others in banding together into pressure groups and a variety of these were formed in the nineteen sixties both for and against reorganization. However, only a very small percentage of parents joined such groups and the vast majority remained apathetic and uninvolved. This was probably to the great relief of most LEAs as what is apparent from these studies is the general lack of commitment on the part of most members and officers to increased parental participation. For a variety of reasons, discussed earlier, opportunities for participation and the timely release of necessary information were usually absent. What consultation there was being largely to explain and defend rather than to listen and learn. Only in a very few LEAs did the style of politics encourage genuine public debate. Ironically, parents were most successful when they exerted their pressure not directly on their LEA but indirectly through the DES.

Attempts to bring influence to bear through using the courts did little other than to highlight the very limited powers of parents laid down in law. Adequate consultation as defined by the courts never amounted to much and in the end the power of decision was left firmly in the hands of the authorities. A series of procedural battles may have served to delay change or force authorities to play more closely according to the rules but there was never any doubt who was going to win the war — especially as the central authorities could always change the rules if needs be!

There was little evidence of members or officers attaching much importance to the need to take account of parental opinions. On the contrary such opinions were often seen as representing a challenge to the autonomy, legitimacy and professionalism of the formal decision makers. In the circumstances it was always tempting to write off such opinions as divided, shifting, narrow and ill-informed. The development of political parties seems to have done little to alter this situation. Decision making has become increasingly closed and centralized and parental opinion is not generally seen as a potent electoral influence. Whatever lip service is paid to the ideal most

LEAs lack both the machinery and the tradition of meaningful consultation with parents. What is more few of them have any real commitment to involving parents any more than they have to. The influence of teachers was greater as a result of their assumed expertise, their greater strategic importance to the authority, and the developed tradition and machinery for teacher consultation. Furthermore, secondary reorganization had obvious career implications as well as raising major educational issues. LEAs needed the cooperation of teachers and teachers were naturally concerned with the adequacy of building and staffing arrangements in any reorganization scheme. In the light of all this it would have been surprising if evidence of teacher consultation was not much greater than in the case of parents and so it was. Working usually through unions teachers were represented on a wide variety of working parties and committees. But the existence of consultation does not imply a corresponding influence and much seemed to depend on how significant their views were to CEOs and members of education committees and these varied sharply. Also important was the extent to which the authority was controlled by a single party with strong policy commitments. Where this was the case the teachers' role was limited to bargaining over fairly minor details of schemes. Where, on the other hand, no single party exercized control or where the ruling party was very divided teacher influence was correspondingly greater. The impact of teachers also related to how united and determined they were and this varied. Certainly teacher attitudes both to reorganization in principle and the details of individual schemes were often sharply divided and, to this extent, their bargaining position was weakened. In some instances teachers recognizing this deliberately succeeded in sinking their differences and presented a united front. Where they did this their influence was generally much greater. Not only did it illustrate the importance they attached to the issue but made it more practical for the authorities to work with them in drawing up a workable scheme.

LEAs varied considerably in terms of attitudes towards teacher consultation. With the passage of time authorities appear to attach greater importance to the value of consultation but depending on the views of individual CEOs and leading councillors. In some instances a change of CEO or controlling party served to alter existing traditions. In some authorities comprehensive reorganization itself served to challenge the absence of adequate machinery and brought about major changes. In others the absence of machinery and traditions proved more durable stumbling blocks. Teachers as individual party members occasionally operated as ginger groups persuading others of the need for change and highlighting what they saw as the weaknesses of the existing system. But generally teachers were not initiators of change. When their voice was raised it was usually in reaction to the initiatives of others.

Future research could well focus on councillors' attitudes towards participation and their perceptions of pressure groups, how they categorize them and react to them. Even where the existence of conflicting interests is acknowledged it remains possible that councillors may regard themselves as constituting a sufficient cross-section of the public to reflect and resolve such conflicts themselves without any need for outside consultation. Studies such as Dearlove's (1973) have suggested that councillors' reactions to pressure groups are highly selective depending on the nature of groups, their demands and their methods of demand articulation. We need to know about councillors' sources of information and how they grade and evaluate 'external' as against 'internal' opinions. There is a need for more information about the membership of different groups, the sorts of issues which stimulate their political activity, the means they adopt and the determinants of their success or failure. We cannot assume that a model of 'group struggle' is useful until we have a better idea of what groups are active in local politics and under what conditions their activity can become an important determinant of policy. The relationship between local parties and groups remains largely unexplored as does the impact of different types of party system on pressure group activity. Kogan (1975) has gone some way towards analysing and categorizing educational pressure groups at national level but there has been no equivalent study at local level.

Political Parties

Opinions vary on the importance of local parties in policy making and part of the explanation for this lies in the variability of party systems. In some authorities a highly developed party system ensures the ruling party enjoys a near monopoly of control over policy issues. Such systems seem increasingly likely to develop in the reorganized system of local government though there was evidence of their extension even before reorganization. Over the particular issue of secondary reorganization the influence of party, not surprisingly, has been particularly acute though it would be wrong to exclude other factors. Thus, by no means all Labour controlled councils were wholly sympathetic to reorganization any more than all Conservative councils were utterly opposed. Often the divisions within the parties were as striking as those between them and both major parties locally as well as nationally have been ambivalent in their attitudes. In the light of such uncertainty educational arguments as voiced by CEOs, parents and teachers, factors such as resource availability and the example of other authorities all had their influence. Nevertheless, the extent of this influence did tend to vary by the degree to which the local party was disciplined and determined. Within such disciplined systems the real power usually rested with a very small group of the most senior councillors in the ruling party. This power being conceived of in terms of both initiating and carrying through their own policy inclinations and acting as filters through which the initiatives of others had to pass. They thus played a central role in determining policy outcomes. In systems where parties were less highly developed other centres of control and initiative tended to develop, notably among the officers.

A striking feature of local parties was their degree of autonomy. As has already been noted the degree of electoral and pressure group opinion is not as great as is frequently assumed. Attempts by the national parties to control the policies of their local counterparts met with mixed results. Likewise the degree of influence supporters of the party can bring to bear on elected members is limited. The relationship between the local party and the party group on the council allows the latter considerable freedom of action and it would be quite wrong to see them merely as mouthpieces of local party activists. Furthermore within the party group evidence suggests control over policy making is even more centralized within a very small number of leading councillors. Quite often the initiative for reorganization developed in the actions of small numbers of individuals within local Labour groups who persuaded leading members of the party to adopt their ideas. The extent to which opposition parties, teachers and parents were involved depended very much on the attitudes of leading members of the majority party and the traditions within that party. It also depended on the attitudes of these other groups to reorganization. Where they were not opposed in principle their degree of involvement and influence was greater. In other instances the majority party pursued its policies with little regard for opposition parties or any other groups.

In discussing the influence of party on local policy making it is essential to remember the variability of party systems within local government. Parties vary in the degree of discipline and solidarity they exhibit, the extent to which power is centralized or dispersed, the degree to which they develop and promote their own policies or those of others notably officers, the importance they attach to policy making as against their other functions, the extent to which they are in a competitive or one party system, the relative power positions of such key individuals as the party leader and committee chairmen. Some of these characteristics reflect differences between the traditions and structures of the Conservative and Labour parties. Thus there is evidence that local Labour parties tend to be the more disciplined and policy oriented of the two, and to attach greater importance to limiting the influence of officers on policy decisions. In addition ideological divergencies between the parties relating to the proper role of government and the relative priorities and interpretations to be given conflicting values such as educational opportunity, freedom of choice and standards of excellence, are also important in explaining attitudes to secondary reorganization. Too many studies talk glibly about the importance of parties in policy making without identifying which elements within the party are important and subject to what conditions.

The case studies clearly show parties as playing a crucial role in policy making. The nature of the local party system had major impacts on relations with central government, local pressure groups and officers' roles. Yet, the only specific study of political parties in local government is Bulpitt's valuable but now outdated (1967) work. Not only was this based on research carried out in the period 1955-1960 but is limited to a sample of boroughs in the north-west of England. No major study has since focussed exclusively on the role of parties in local government and what references there have been deal mainly with parties as electoral devices. We know little about their role in aggregating community opinions or the dynamics of the policy making process within them though valuable work has been done by Jennings (1977). Because the meetings of party groups are not usually open to researchers we know very little about how these operate. We need to know more about the relations between local and national parties and within local parties the relations between rank and file members and the party group on the council. As parties now dominate the selection of councillors we need to explore how they recruit and socialize members. Dearlove (1973) has pioneered work in this area but very little has been done since. In particular, we need major research into the effects of local government reorganization on styles of local politics. Nearly all the available literature refers to parties in the old system and may be misleading if applied uncritically to the present situation.

Councillors and Officers

Studies of councillors confirm the crucial importance of such determinants of behaviour as party affiliations and role conceptions. They also underline the fact that both the machinery of party and councillors' own self-conceptions of role result in policy making remaining in the hands of very few people. As a general rule, the significance of committee chairmen and party leaders is confirmed.

We now have a considerable body of information on the roles and role conceptions of councillors but most of this relates to pre-reorganization and pre-Bains authorities and it would be useful to discover what changes, if any, have taken place more recently. The construction of typologies of councillors is of value in helping to understand policy making though it can become an end in itself. To date the main value of these typologies has been in alerting us to the diversity of roles members perform. Particularly important are the implications of different roles in terms of members' attitudes to party, constituents, pressure groups and policy making. We also need to know more about the determinants of role orientations such as the influence of seniority and party affiliations.

Several of the case studies show the initiative for secondary reorganization coming from leading councillors. In other instances determined groups of councillors withstood pressure from the DES, parent and teacher groups to reorganize. Councillors are thus in a strong position to initiate, amend and veto policy developments. Their power, however, is shared with officers and this is the area where our detailed knowledge is least satisfactory. We know the relationship is infinitely variable due to factors of individual personality. Also the significance of officers' contribution to policy varies inversely with the degree of party cohesion and control. In this context Hill (1972) has made a valuable distinction between ideological and administrative politics which, unfortunately, has not been taken up and developed in any of the empirical work. The case studies do not provide much evidence of CEOs playing as dominant a role as is often suggested. The initiative usually developed within the majority party which then requested officers to draw up alternative schemes to achieve their ends. In drawing up such alternatives officers needed to be mindful of their likely acceptability to party leaders and their room for manoeuvre was always limited. Where CEOs failed to tailor their proposals sufficiently closely to party requirements they were usually rejected. Only where parties were weakly developed, inexperienced, divided or lacking political will was a vacuum created which CEOs could fill with their own ideas. Even here some CEOs failed to step in and awaited changes in the political situation before acting. Generally CEOs played a reactive role and many of them avoided giving a strong lead either for or against change. Instead they tended to adopt a low profile taking their lead from whatever party happened to hold the majority. This may reflect the highly politicized nature of the issue but such reticence is still surprising given the considerable educational importance of the issue.

None of the studies of secondary reorganization however go very far in forwarding our understanding of this crucial area. All we discover is the variability of the relationship with little by way of explanation apart from the above. It is difficult to disagree with the following comment:

> Within the study of local government in the UK remarkably little is known about how bureaucrats interact with each other, with politicians, what they interact about and under what circumstances: we know even less about the consequences of those interactions (Greenwood *et al*, 1972).

Research into officer-member relations is probably the most difficult area of all and many otherwise perceptive studies have been forced to fall back on the usual cliches. Views by the participants themselves are available but raise problems of validity and representativeness.

Outsiders rarely succeed in persuading officers to divulge much and usually rely on members' interpretations. Books on local government management abound with prescriptive statements on the issue and political texts rehearse the arguments for and against 'rule by the permanent officials'. But actual case studies which provide any detailed insight into the relationship are almost non-existent. It is, therefore, much easier to document areas of research than to suggest how such work might be successfully undertaken. Such areas should include the role of officers as information gatekeepers, relations between officers and parties and pressure groups, officers' role conceptions and role conflicts, the tactics of persuasion, and the ways roles differ by the nature of what is being discussed. The question is not whether officers or members determine policy. They both do and the question is in what ways do they do so and how and why does this vary. The idea of partnership between officers and members can be misleading in that it distracts attention from the fact that each side is likely to see issues from different perspectives and to be influenced by different pressures. We know next to nothing about the detailed interactions between CEOs and education chairmen, about how policy options emerge and are evaluated within departments, about interactions between education officers and other departments, about the ideological and professional assumptions of officers and their socializing influences over members.

Methodology

Having discussed possible areas of research it is now necessary to consider the question of methodology. It is notable that all the available studies of reorganization have used the case study method usually focussing on events in a single authority. It is appropriate, therefore, to consider this technique attempting to discern its strengths and weaknesses. If in doing so I am harsh in my judgement of the studies which have proved of such use to me I hope this will be interpreted in the spirit in which it is intended; namely, to promote critical thinking about future work in this area.

At the moment, students of local policy making fall into what are almost two rival camps. Those who proceed by case studies and those who deny case studies can prove anything and see as more 'scientific' the analysis of aggregate statistical data covering large numbers of authorities. This latter approach builds upon work pioneered in America by Dye (1966) and in Britain the main proponents are Alt, Boaden and Davies (1968, 1969, 1971, 1972). Such studies typically use as indicators of policy, variations in expenditure per head of population over a series of local authorities. There are, however, major problems in interpreting such variations which may in part reflect differences in prices, in the use of resources, in levels of efficiency, or methods of data collection and presentation. Additionally, there is much more to local policy than expenditure patterns and there is considerable scope for variance in decisions not directly reflected in spending. Some key policy changes have only minor, if any, expenditure effects and financial constraints may divert political efforts into just those policy changes having least expenditure impact. Statistical studies impose strict methodological requirements if their findings are to be valuable. Furthermore, statistical association does not compensate for the approach's lack of explanatory linkages. As Dearlove (1973, p.69) summarizes 'We are not really offered hypotheses which suggest *why* we can expect these associations and neither are we told just *how* it is that certain socio-economic conditions are translated into public policies by the structure of government'. It is here that statistical studies need to be complemented by individual case studies which explore in detail the workings of the policy making process.

The use of the case study as a technique for studying local policy making is well established and has good supporting arguments. Perhaps above all, it enables the researcher to get the feel of a particular political system through the close observation of events. It encourages an understanding of situations more tangible than broad generalizations offer, by showing how situations are understood by the actors themselves. This is particularly important in enabling the researcher to go some way towards understanding the way participants conceive of the world in which they operate. Creating models and theories involves abstracting certain features from situations and generalizing about a limited range of relationships. By contrast, case studies show something of the great variations and complexities of situations and serve as a foil to the search for theories and generalizations. They also have the appeal that they are often interesting to conduct, fairly manageable for a single researcher, and there are plenty of examples on which to base one's own attempt. In terms of technical tools they can integrate a wide range of data including existing historical material, aggregate quantitative data, interviews and sample surveys.

Traditionally as Heclo (1972, p.89) points out 'the most widespread use of case studies has been in the hands of those whose primary interest is pedagogic rather than theoretical'. In this connection it has undoubted value, but its use as a research tool to develop theory and test hypotheses has provoked a more mixed response. Opinions divide between those who hold that if used carefully the method can advance theory and those who argue that it cannot however carefully it is used. The latter viewpoint is held by those who believe that political understanding can only develop through the use of statistical studies covering a very large number of cases. We have already considered this approach and argued that it needs to be complemented by the use of case studies. There is little doubt that case studies by the insight they provide can generate hypotheses but can they be used to test them? Obviously case studies can disprove a hypothesis by showing it to be out of accord with the 'facts'. They can sort out plausible from implausible hypotheses. But can a hypothesis actually be proved by case studies? The answer must depend on the degree of specificity of the hypothesis and the number of case studies as a proportion of the total of such cases — obviously a single study cannot alone prove a hypothesis, unless that hypothesis relates only to that single incident. To the extent hypotheses are often imprecise and difficult to operationalize, and to the extent case studies are often isolated events, their value in confirming hypotheses is limited. But this is not to argue that there is something inherently atheoretical about the use of case studies. Rather the argument is that much depends on the way the studies are conducted. In particular we must guard against the assumption that theoretical advance will automatically result from the creation of more and more case studies.

Certainly a number of problems are linked with the use of this method. One, which advocates of the analysis of aggregate data focus on, being the extent to which one can generalize from such studies. This is not only a question of the number of such studies as a proportion of the total universe but the extent to which the choice of issue partly determines the conclusions reached. Also, to the extent the method focuses on particular decisions the whole area of non-decision making and policy maintenance risks being ignored. Almost inevitably case studies tend to examine instances of change and may ignore or underestimate the forces which encourage the continuation of existing policies and serve to keep demands for change off the political agenda. Case studies through their reliance on interviews with individuals and group leaders may overemphasize their importance compared with overall structural factors such as the influence of central government, economic conditions and implicit biases within the decision making system itself. There may also be a tendency to give a neatness to the narrative, a clear beginning and end, which fails to portray the complexity and untidiness of most policy processes. Even worse is the temptation to force the data to fit some preconceived hypothesis by excluding non-supportive data.

The whole question of information access and the selective willingness of respondents to help the researcher poses major difficulties. Attempts to study policy decisions depend very much on a minimum of cooperation from the particular authority involved. Much hinges on the attitudes of CEOs and education chairmen who often feel obliged to maintain a veil of secrecy especially over controversial decisions. Compared to his counterpart in the United States the British researcher has far greater difficulty getting access to official information. Even where confidential files are made available this may be linked to some degree of censorship over what may subsequently be published. Thus the authors of one set of local case studies (Donnison *et al.*, 1975, p.45) comment: 'Publication had then to be approved by senior officials, and at times is seemed that our studies were either dull, because we had not discovered the full story or unpublishable — because we had'. Even where individuals are prepared to give unconditional assistance their recollection of events is likely to be partial and biased. The researcher is almost always faced with rival recollections and interpretations of events and has the unenviable task of producing his own version out of a mass of conflicting viewpoints and emphases. Apart from interviews with officers, members, party spokesmen, teacher, parent and other group representatives minutes and reports of various kinds may provide additional material. However, access to these will have to be negotiated and by glossing over the more subtle disagreements that preceeded decisions they may conceal as much as they reveal.

The absence of a generally agreed framework or model into which to fit and compare case study findings is a particular problem. Case studies can be aimless exercizes merely illustrating no better what is already well illustrated and producing no insights to stimulate further inquiries. We need studies which examine the nature of local policy making in terms of theoretical models. Lindblom's (1963 and 1965) model of decision making as disjointed incrementalism suggests a number of dimensions along which policy developments could be analysed. Questions which the model draws attention to include the following. Was the policy adopted incremental in that it represented the least possible modification to existing policy? What were the goals of the various decision makers and how were these changed and reconciled over time? Does incrementalism describe with reasonable accuracy the way policy was made and does it commend itself as a prescriptive model of what decision making should be like? Similar lists could be produced for systems* theory with its useful concepts of environmental demands and supports, conversion and feedback processes, gatekeepers and so on or from the model of Vickers (1965) with his insightful concepts of appreciative behaviour and regulating, optimizing and balancing functions. The object is not to test the validity of these theories as to use them to generate hypotheses, to draw attention to situations that need explanation and to provide a vocabulary for discussing issues more coherently and systematically. A major criticism of the case studies of secondary reorganization is the general failure to draw upon this body of literature. As a result each study has tended to be exhaustively and excessively descriptive and in this respect often a painstaking exercize. What has been missing has been the attempt to do more than an historical exercize — and even historians are now increasingly analytical and theoretical in their approach. Very few studies made any attempt to apply incrementalism or systems theory. Even simple references to pluralism or elitism were uncommon. In addition most writers

---

*Examples of the use of a systems perspective to analyse educational policy making in Britain include a study of the introduction of B. Ed. degrees in six English universities and a study of the ILEA's review of post school provision. Both are unpublished London University Ph.D.'s but summaries can be found in D. A. Howell's 'Systems Analysis and Academic Decision Making in Universities', *Educational Administration*, Spring 1976, and R. J. Brown's Research Report: Systems Analysis and Decision Making in the Local Government of Further Education', *Educational Administration*, Summer 1978. A much more limited attempt to examine some of the case study material on secondary reorganization from a systems standpoint is P. M. Ribbins and R. J. Brown (1979).

seemed unaware of the wider literature on local government. References to works dealing generally with the roles of parties, pressure groups, members and officers and central-local relations were extraordinarily sparse. Most surprising of all was the seeming unawareness of other studies of secondary reorganization. Hardly any of the studies refer to comparable work done elsewhere despite the availability of such material. Each researcher seems to have proceeded using his own methods and produced a largely personal account of events. This policy of 'splendid isolation' cannot be expected to lead to a greater and systematic understanding of local policy making. The mere creation of more and more case studies without a coherent theoretical base and merely itemizing the idiosyncracies of individual local education authorities is a sad waste of research resources.

Most of the studies were based on events in a single authority. Future studies should attempt to look at a number of authorities either of a similar or contrasting nature. Nearly all the studies examined events over a very limited period of time. A more balanced picture would be derived from the study of local education authorities over long periods allowing the discernment of trends and putting specific events into their historical context. The study of an extended series of decisions and events enables us to give fuller consideration to feedback processes and changes in the economic and political environment. Policy becomes not a simple dependent output but a dynamic independent variable acting on other variables over time. Relationships between the main participants in educational policy making have not remained constant over time. Several writers have suggested a tightening of central control. Others have pointed to a change in the relationship between education and other services within local authorities. Changes in the party system and management structures have major implications for the relationships between officers and members. The study of decision making over a prolonged period of time is far more likely to increase our understanding of such developments than a study limited to a single point in time. Nearly all the reorganization studies stop at the point a reorganization plan is finally approved and very little work has been done on the process of implementation and the impact on the locality. Few studies relate developments at the local level to broader national developments both political and economic. Thus many of the studies appeared isolated both in time and space.

In addition very few studies attempt to divide the policy making process into different stages such as problem awareness and identification, formulation of alternative policies, analysis and selection of alternatives, policy implementation and adjustment. The value of such a model being to draw attention to the different questions that may be posed at the various stages. It also directs attention to the possibility that the influence of different individuals and groups may vary according to the particular stage in the process being analysed. Thus, for example, Jennings (1977) has argued that officers are particularly influential at the level of problem identification and the generation of alternative policies while committee chairmen play a more crucial role at the stage of choosing between alternatives.

In America the trend is away from studies of single authorities and towards the study of large numbers of communities. In Britain the trend has been towards in-depth studies of particular cities. These have been valuable but until we know how such cities fit into the general pattern of local government they are of limited value as far as generalizations are concerned. What we need are broad comparative studies to ground and inform more detailed case studies. The trouble with much of the work being done is that studies do not build upon one another.

The emphasis on studies of comprehensive reorganization is understandable given its significance both educationally and politically. Nevertheless, it does mean that our in-depth studies of local educational policy making are almost entirely limited to this one area. This is unfortunate because as an area it is so untypical, given the high degree of political conflict it evoked. This suggests that it would be unwise to make unqualified generalizations from these case studies about the roles of central government, parties, pressure groups or members and officers. The nature of the political system, in so far as we are able to perceive it, is partly pre-determined by the nature of the issues through which we choose to examine it. What these studies show is how such groups operate when dealing with highly politicized issues. This is not without value but what we also need are studies of decision making in more routine areas of education which may make less exciting reading and research but do more to further our understanding of how LEAs more typically make and implement policy.

It is also notable that nearly all studies are of urban authorities, notably old county boroughs and we have very little material on policy making patterns in rural areas. This is unfortunately true of local government studies generally where we have major studies of authorities in London (Rhodes, 1972; Wistrich, 1972; Dearlove, 1973), Wolverhampton (Jones, 1969), Leeds (Wiseman, 1967), Sheffield (Hampton, 1970) and Birmingham (Newton, 1976) but very little by way of rural areas (Lee, 1963, Madgwick *et al.*, 1974). Even studies which attempt to sample a number of different authorities manage to avoid rural areas. Thus Sharpe's (1967) study of local elections focuses exclusively on municipal elections, Boaden's (1971) work on county boroughs and Bulpitt's (1967) on boroughs and county boroughs. We have hardly any studies relating to educational policy making in Wales, Scotland or Northern Ireland. With hardly a single exception the available studies of secondary reorganization relate exclusively to English local authorities. Very few studies set out to compare decision making in different authorities. In short, the considerable opportunities for the comparative study of local policy making in the United Kingdom have yet to be grasped. A good deal of the problem is the absence of collaborative research. So long as the tradition of the solitary researcher with limited time and funds continues the only comparative research is likely to be on a very limited scale and the tendency will be for a continuation of isolated single authority studies.

Apart from this plea for more wide ranging comparative work it is likely that case studies in general will be more effective if the following considerations are born in mind. The need for some conceptual framework which suggests certain questions which the studies are concerned to answer. This gives them a focus other than simple narrative. Case studies should build upon one another so that some degree of generalization is possible and where variations are discovered hypotheses can be developed to account for these. The study of local authorities gives considerable opportunities for this kind of replication but if there is no shared conceptual framework or awareness of other studies the benefits are largely illusory. Serious attention needs to be given to the full variety of data available. Sometimes case studies focus too narrowly on the use of interview and press material ignoring such useful data as records of local expenditure, population characteristics, voting figures over a period of time, sample surveys and existing historical studies. There is a danger of ignoring general environmental factors apart from those with obvious political connotations. The selection of topics for case studies should focus on the normal and typical rather than the dramatic and exceptional. Whatever the appeal of the latter for teaching purposes their value for the generation and testing of hypotheses is limited. There should be a concentration on cases dealing with the same or similar phenomena so that the same variables can be observed and compared. There should be a clear research design covering what data is to be collected and in what form. To assist this researchers should be aware of existing hypotheses in the area of public policy studies so that research is not undertaken at random but in relation to existing theory. So used, the case study is a research tool which despite limitations has clear advantages in the analysis of public policy making.

References and Bibliography

ALT, J. (1971). 'Some Social and Political Correlates of County Borough Expenditures'. *Brit. J. of Pol. Sci.,* **1**, 3, 49-63.

ASHFORD, D.E. (1974). 'The Effects of Central Finance on the British Local Government System', *Brit. J. of Pol. Sci.,* **4**, 3, 305-22.

AULD, R. (1976). *William Tyndale Infants and Junior School Public Inquiry.* London: ILEA.

BACON, W. (1978). *Public Accountability and the Schooling System.* London: Harper & Row.

BARKER, R. (1972). *Education and Politics 1900-1951.* Oxford University Press.

BARON, G. and HOWELL, D.A. (1974). *The Government and Management of Schools.* London: Athlone Press.

BATLEY, R., O'BRIEN, O. and PARRIS, H. (1970). *Going Comprehensive.* London: Routledge & Kegan Paul.

BEALEY, F.J., BLONDEL, J. and McCANN, W.P. (1965). *Constituency Politics.* London: Faber.

BEER, S. (1965). *Modern British Politics.* London: Faber.

BELL, R. (Ed) (1973). *Education in Great Britain and Jreland.* London: Routledge & Kegan Paul.

BENN, C. and SIMON, B. (1972). *Half Way There.* (2nd edn). Harmondsworth: Penguin.

BENN, C. (1974). 'Education in Committee', *New Society,* **27**, 507-8.

BILSKI, R. (1973) 'Ideology and the Comprehensive Schools', *Pol. Quarterly,* **44**, 197-211.

BIRCH, A.H. (1959). *Small Town Politics.* Oxford University Press.

BIRLEY, D. (1970). *The Education Officer and His World.* London: Routledge & Kegan Paul.

BOADEN, N. (1970). 'Central Departments and Local Authorities: The relationship re-examined', *Pol. Studies,* **18**, 2, 175-86.

BOADEN, N. (1971). *Urban Policy Making.* Cambridge University Press.

BOADEN, N. and ALFORD, R.R. (1969). 'Sources of Diversity in English Local Government Decisions', *Public Admin.,* **47**, 203-23.

BOYLE, E. (1972). 'The Politics of Secondary School Reorganisation. Some reflections'. *J. of Educ. Admin. and History,* **4**, 28-38.

BRAND, J. (1965). 'Ministry Control and Local Autonomy in Education',
    Pol. Quarterly, **36,** 154-163.
BRAYBROOKE, D. and LINDBLOM, C.E. (1963). *A Strategy of Decision.*
    New York: The Free Press.
BRIER, A. (1970). 'The Decision Process in Local Government'. *Public
    Admin.* **48,** 153-68.
BULPITT, J.G. (1967). *Party Politics in English Local Government.*
    Harlow: Longmans.
BUXTON, R. (1970). *Local Government.* Harmondsworth: Penguin.
CLEMENTS, R.V. (1969). *Local Notables and the City Council.* London:
    MacMillan.
COATES, R.D. (1972). *Teachers' Unions and Interest Group Politics.* Cam-
    bridge University Press.
CORBETT, A. (1970). 'Comprehensives: "the tally", *New Society,* **15,** 264-6.
CORINA, L. (1974). 'Elected Representatives in a Party System: A
    Typology', *Policy and Politics,* **3,** 1, 69-87.
COUSINS, P.F. (1976). 'Voluntary Organisations and Local Government
    in three South London Boroughs', *Public Admin.,* **54,** 63-81.
CRISPIN, A. (1976). 'Local Government Finance: Assessing the Central
    Government's Contributuion', *Public Admin.,* **54,** 45-62.
DARK, A.C. (1967). An Historical study of Secondary Reorganisation in
    England and Wales up to 1965, with special reference to Bradford.
    Unpublished M.Ed. dissertation, University of Durham.
DARKE, R. and WALKER (Eds) (1977). *Local Government and the Public.*
    London: Leonard Hill.
DAVID, M.E. (1977). *Reform, Reaction and Resources.* Slough: NFER.
DAVIES, B. (1968). *Social Needs and Resources in Local Services.* London:
    Michael Joseph.
DAVIES, B. (1969). 'Local Authority Size: some associations with standards
    of performance of services for deprived children and old people'.
    Public Admin. **47,** 225-48.
DAVIES, B., BARTON, A., McMILLAN, I., and WILLIAMSON, V.
    (1971). *Variations in services for the Aged.* London: Bell.
DAVIES, B. (1972). *Variations in Children's services among British Urban
    Authorities.* London: Bell.
DAVIES, J.G. (1972). *The Evangelistic Bureaucrat.* London: Tavistock.
DEARLOVE, J. (1973). *The Politics of Policy in Local Government.*
    Cambridge University Press.
DEPARTMENT OF EDUCATION AND SCIENCE (1977). *A New
    Partnership for Our Schools.* (Taylor Report) London: HMSO.
DEPARTMENT OF EDUCATION AND SCIENCE (1979). *Aspects of
    Secondary Education in England. A Survey by HM Inspectors of
    Schools.* London: HMSO.
DEPARTMENT OF THE ENVIRONMENT (1972). *The New Local
    Authorities: management and structure.* (Bains Report) London:
    HMSO.
DONNISON, D.V. and CHAPMAN, V. (1975). *Social Policy and
    Administration Revisited.* London: Allen & Unwin.
DYE, T.R. (1966). *Politics, Economics and the Public.* Rand McNally.

EASTON, D. (1965). *A Systems Analysis of Political Life.* New York: John Wiley & Sons.

ECCLES, P.R. (1971). The Reorganisation of secondary education in Tynemouth 1963-70: An examination of the problems and processes of implementation. Unpublished MA dissertation, Leeds University.

ECCLES, P.R. (1974). 'Secondary Reorganisation in Tynemouth 1962-69', *J. of Educ. Admin. and History,* **1,** 35-45.

ECKSTEIN, H. (1960). *Pressure Group Politics.* London: Allen & Unwin.

EGGLESTON, S.J. (1966). 'Going Comprehensive', *New Society,* **221,** 944-6.

FEARN, E. (1977). Role of political parties and pressure groups in comprehensive reorganisation in four local education areas: Chesterfield, Doncaster, Rotherham and Sheffield. Unpublished Ph.D. dissertation, Leeds University.

FENWICKE, I.G.K. (1967). Organised opinion and the comprehensive school: a study of some educational groups and the policy making process for education in England. Unpublished Ph.D. dissertation, Manchester University.

FENWICKE, I.G.K. (1976). *The Comprehensive School 1944-1970.* London: Methuen.

FENWICKE, I.G.K. and WOODTHORPE, A.J. (1980). 'The Reorganisation of Secondary Education in Leeds: the role of committee chairmen and political parties'. *Aspects of Education* (forthcoming).

GOSDEN, P.H.J.H. (1976). *Education in the Second World War.* London: Methuen.

GREENWOOD, R. and HININGS, C.R. (1977). 'The study of Local Government: Towards an organisational Analysis', *Public Admin. Bull.* **23,** 2, 15.

GREGORY, R. (1969). 'Local Elections and the Rule of Anticipated Reactions', *Pol. Studies,* **17,** 31-47.

GRIFFITH, J.A.G. (1966). *Central Departments and Local Authorities.* London: Allen & Unwin.

GRIFFITHS, A. (1971). *Secondary School Reorganisation in England and Wales.* London: Routledge & Kegan Paul.

HALSALL, E. (1973). *The Comprehensive School; guidelines for the reorganisation of secondary education.* Oxford: Pergamon.

HAMPTON, W. (1970). *Democracy and Community.* Oxford University Press.

HARTLEY, O.A. (1971). 'The Relations between central and local authorities', *Public Admin.,* **49,** 439-56.

HECLO, H.H. (1969). 'The Councillor's Job', *Public Admin.,* **47,** 185-202.

HECLO, H.H. (1972). 'Review Article: Policy Analysis'. *Brit. J. of Pol. Sci.,* **2,** 1, 83.108-

HECLO, H.H. (1974). *Modern Social Politics in Britain and Sweden.* Yale University Press.

HECLO, H.H. and WILDAVSKY, A. (1974). *The Private Government of Public Money.* London: MacMillan.

HEIDENHEIMER, H.J. and PARKINSON, M. (1975). Equalising Education and Opportunity in Britain and USA. *Tulane University, Studies in Pol. Sci.,* **15**.

HEWITSON, J.N. (1969). *The Grammar School Tradition in a Comprehensive World.* London: Routledge & Kegan Paul.

HILL, D.M. (1974). *Democratic Theory and Local Government.* London: Allen & Unwin.

HILL, D.M. (1970). *Participating in Local Affairs.* London: Penguin.

HILL, M.J. (1972) *The Sociology of Public Administration.* London: Weidenfeld & Nicholson.

HOWELL, D.A. (1978). *A Bibliography of Educational Administration in the United Kingdom.* Slough: NRFER.

ISAAC-HENRY, K. (1970). The Politics of Comprehensive Education in Birmingham, 1957-67. Unpublished MSc. dissertation, Birmingham University.

JENNINGS, R.E. (1975). 'Political Perspectives on Local Government Re-organisation', *Local Government Studies,* **1**, 4, 21-37.

JENNINGS, R.E. (1977). *Education and Politics: policy making in local education authorities.* London: Batsford.

JOHNSON, N. (1965). 'Who are the Policy Makers?', *Public Admin.,* **43**, 281-7.

JONES, G.W. (1969). *Borough Politics.* London: MacMillan.

JONES, G.W. (1973). 'The Functions and Organisation of Councillors', *Public Admin.,* **51**, 135-46.

JONES, G.W. (1973). 'Political Leadership in Local Government, *Local Government Studies,* **5**, 1-11.

JONES, G.W. (1975). 'Varieties of Local Politics', *Local Government Studies,* **1**, 2, 17-32.

KANTOR, P. (1976). 'Elites, Pluralists and Policy Areas in London', *Brit. J.of Pol. Sci.,* **6**, 311-34.

KEITH-LUCAS, B. (1961). *The Councils, the Press and the People.* Conservative and Unionist Central Office.

KOGAN, M. (1971). *The Politics of Education: Interviews with Crosland and Boyle.* Harmondsworth: Penguin.

KOGAN, M. with Van der EYKEN, W. (1973). *County Hall: The Role of the Chief Education Officer.* Harmondsworth: Penguin.

KOGAN, M. (1975). *Educational Policy Making.* London: Allen & Unwin.

LEE, J.M. (1963). *Social Leaders and Public Persons.* Oxford University Press.

LEWIN, R.R. (1968). Secondary School Reorganisation in the Outer London Boroughs with special reference to the London Borough of Merton. Unpublished M.A. dissertation, University of London.

LINDBOLM, C.E. (1965). *The Intelligence of Democracy: Decision Making through Mutual Adjustment.* New York: Free Press.

LOCKE, M. (1974). *Power and Politics in the School System.* London: Routledge & Kegan Paul.

MACKENZIE, M.L. (1967). 'The road to the Circulars', *Scottish Educ. Studies,* **1**, 1, 25-33.

MANDER, J.A. (1975). Freedom and Constraint in a Local Authority. Unpublished Ph.D. dissertation, Leicester University.

MADGWICK, P.J., GRIFFITHS, N. and WALKER, V. (1974). *The Politics of Rural Wales: a study of Cardiganshire.* London: Hutchinson.
MANZER, R.A. (1970). *Teachers and Politics.* Manchester University Press.
MARCH, J.G. and SIMON H.A. (1958). *Organisations.* New York: Wiley & Sons.
MARMION, V.J.S. (1967). A Study of Interests in educational administration in Liverpool. Unpublished MA dissertation, Liverpool University.
MINISTRY OF HOUSING AND LOCAL GOVERNMENT (1967). *Committee on the Management of Local Government (Maud Report)* London: HMSO. Vol. 1: Report of the Committee; Vol. 2: The Local Government Councillor; Vol. 5: Local Government Administration in England and Wales.
NEVE, B. (1977). 'Bureaucracy and Politics in Local Government: The Role of Local Authority Education Officers', *Public Admin.,* **55.** 291-303.
NEWTON, K. (1976). *Second City Politics.* Oxford University Press.
OLIVER, F.R. and STANYER, J. (1969). 'Some aspects of the Financial Behaviour of County Boroughs', *Public Admin.,* **47,** 169-84.
PARKINSON, M. (1970). *The Labour Party and the Organisation of Secondary Education 1918-1965.* London: Routledge & Kegan Paul.
PARKINSON, M. (1971). 'Central Local Relations in British Parties: A local view', *Pol. Studies,* **19,** 4, 440-6.
PARKINSON, M. (1972). *Politics of Urban Education.* University of Liverpool.
PARTINGTON, J.A. (1975). 'Secondary Reorganisation and the Courts of Law', *J. of Educ. Admin. and History,* **7,** 40-4.
PEDLEY, R. (1978). *The Comprehensive School.* Harmondsworth: Penguin.
PESCHEK, D. and BRAND, J.A. (1966). *Policies and Politics in Secondary Education.* Greater London Papers No. 11, London School of Economics.
PETERSON, P.E. (1971). 'British Interest Group Theory Re-examined: the Politics of Comprehensive Education in three British Cities', *Comparative Politics,* **3,** 3, 381-402.
PETERSON, P.E. and KANTOR, P. (1977). 'Political Parties and Citizen Participation in English City Politics', *Comparative Politics,* **19,** 197-217.
PETTIGREW, A.M. (1972). 'Information control as a Power Resource', *Sociology,* **6,** 187-204.
PILE, W. (1979). *The Department of Education and Science.* London: Allen & Unwin.
PRITCHARD, M. (1977), 'Which Scheme? Oxford City Council's Debate on Comprehensive Reorganisation, 1964-67', *Oxford Rev. of Educ.,* **3,** 3, 257-68.
REGAN, D. (1977). *Local Government and Education.* London: Allen & Unwin.
RHODES, G. (Ed) (1972). *The New Government of London, the First Five*

Years. London: Weidenfeld & Nicolson.

RHODES, R.A.W. (1974). A Comparative Study of the Decision Making Process Within Oxford City and Oxfordshire County Councils 1963-68. Unpublished B.Litt. dissertation, Oxford University.

RHODES, R.A.W. (1975). 'The Lost World of British Local Politics', *Local Government Studies*, **13**, 39-59.

RIBBINS, P.M. and BROWN, R.J. (1979). 'Policy Making in English Local Government: The case of Secondary School Reorganisation', *Public Admin.*, **57**, 187-202.

RIGBY, B. (1975). The Planning and Provision of education in the foundation and development of a postwar new town: Crawley, Sussex 1947-66. Unpublished Ph.D. dissertation. Southampton University.

ROSE, R. (1969). 'The Variability of Party Government: a Theoretical and Empirical Critique', *Pol. Studies*, **17**, 4, 413-45.

RUBINSTEIN, D. and SIMON, B. (1973). *The Evolution of the Comprehensive School 1926-72*. London: Routledge & Kegan Paul.

SARAN, R. (1968). Secondary education policy and administration in Middlesex since 1944. Unpublished Ph.D. dissertation, London dissertation.

SARAN, R. (1973). *Policy Making in Secondary Education*. Oxford University Press.

SELF, P. (1971). 'Elected Representatives & Management in Local Government: An Alternative Analysis', *Public Admin.*, **49**, 269-78.

SELF, P. (1972). *Administrative Theories & Politics*. London: Allen & Unwin.

SHARPE, L.J. (Ed) (1967). *Voting in Cities*. London: MacMillan.

SHARPE, L.J. (1973). 'American Democracy Reconsidered', *Brit. J. of Pol. Sci.*, **3**, 1-28, 129-68.

STACEY, M. (1975). *Power, Persistence and Change: A second look at Banbury*. London: Routledge & Kegan Paul.

STANYER, J. (1976). *Understanding Local Government*. London: Fontana.

STERN, M.A. (1971). Policy formation in the Reorganisation of Secondary Schools in Manchester along Comprehensive Lines. Unpublished Diploma in Public Administration dissertation, London University.

SUTCLIFFE, A. and SMITH, R. (1974). *Birmingham 1939-70*. Oxford University Press.

THOMPSON, J. (1952). *Secondary Education Survey: An Analysis of LEA Development Plans*. London: Gollancz.

TURNBULL, J.W. (1969). Secondary Reorganisation in the London Borough of Croydon with special reference to the role of teachers organisations. Unpublished MA dissertation, University of London.

URWIN, K. (1975). 'Formulating a Policy of Secondary Education in Croydon'. In: Donnison, D. and Chapman, V., *Social Policy and Administration Revisited*.

VICKERS, G. (1965). *The Art of Judgement: A study of Policy making*. London: Chapman and Hall.

VICKERS, G. (1974). 'Policy Making in Local government', *Local Government Studies*, **7**, 5-11.

WEBER, M. (1947). *The Theory of Social and Economic Orgnisation.* Oxford University Press.

WHITE, P.T. (1974). The Reorganisation of Secondary Education in Bath and Southampton. Unpublished M.Phil. dissertation, Southampton University.

WISEMAN, H.V. (1967). *Local Government at Work.* London: Routledge & Kegan Paul.

WISTRICH, E. (1972). *Local Government Reorganisation: the first five years of Camden.* London: Borough of Camden.

WOOD, C.A. (1973). Educational Policy in Bristol within the context of National Educational Policy. Unpublished M.Sc. dissertation, Bristol University.

YATES, A. and NEWNES, D.A. (1957). *Admission to Grammar Schools,* Slough: NFER.

Index